P9-CFJ-182

Black Dance
in America

Also by James Haskins

Bill Cosby
America's Most Famous Father

Black Music in America
A History Through Its People

Black Theater in America

Count Your Way Through Africa

Count Your Way Through the Arab World

Count Your Way Through Canada

Count Your Way Through China

Count Your Way Through Japan

Count Your Way Through Korea

Count Your Way Through Mexico

Count Your Way Through Russia

Mr. Bojangles
The Biography of Bill Robinson
(with N. R. Mitgang)

Queen of the Blues
A Biography of Dinah Washington

Shirley Temple Black
Actress to Ambassador

The 60s Reader

Winnie Mandela
Life of Struggle

Black Dance in America

A History Through Its People

Illustrated with photographs

by James Haskins

Thomas Y. Crowell   New York

Acknowledgments

I am grateful to Norma Jean Darden, Ann Kalkhoff, and Arthur Mitchell for their help. A special thank-you to Kathy Benson.

Black Dance in America
Copyright © 1990 by James Haskins
All rights reserved. No part of this book may be
used or reproduced in any manner whatsoever without
written permission except in the case of brief quotations
embodied in critical articles and reviews. Printed in
the United States of America. For information address
Thomas Y. Crowell Junior Books, 10 East 53rd Street,
New York, N.Y. 10022.
Typography by Patricia Tobin

10 9 8 7 6 5 4 3 2 1

First Edition

Library of Congress Cataloging-in-Publication Data
Haskins, James, 1941–
  Black dance in America : a history through its people /
James Haskins.
     p.   cm.
  Bibliography : p.
  Includes index.
  Summary: Surveys the history of black dance in America,
from its beginnings with the ritual dances of African slaves,
through tap and modern dance to break dancing. Includes brief
biographies of influential dancers and companies.
  ISBN 0-690-04657-X : $. — ISBN 0-690-04659-6 (lib. bdg.) :
$
  1. Afro-Americans—Dancing—History—Juvenile literature.
[1. Afro-Americans—Dancing.]   I. Title.
GV1624.7.A34H37 1990   89-35529
792.8′089′96073—dc20   CIP
                                                      AC

To
Virginia,
Jimmy Lee,
Pamela,
and Roger

Contents

Black Dance
in America

Chapter 1
"Dancing the Slaves":
Black Dance Comes to America

When Africans were brought to the New World, they were packed like sardines into the holds of slave ships and forced to endure voyages lasting anywhere from fifteen days to four months, depending on destination and weather at sea. Conditions in the holds were so unsanitary that usually the slaves were stripped naked and their heads shaved so as to prevent the spread of disease. But disease spread anyway, and overcrowding took a terrible toll on the human cargo of the slave ships. Frequently, up to one half died during the voyage.

When weather permitted, the slaves were brought up on deck once a day so that the hold could be cleaned of excrement and vomit. On deck, the slaves "exercised," for slave-ship captains wanted them to look healthy so that they would bring high prices in the New World

slave markets. This exercising was called "dancing the slaves." The slaves were compelled to dance, often prompted with whips. Sometimes, music was provided by a slave beating on a drum or the bottom of a pot, or strumming on the African stringed instrument that white observers variously called a banjo, a banjar, a bangelo, and a bonjour. At other times, a member of the crew would play a bagpipe or fiddle, and slaving captains were known to advertise for sailors who could play a musical instrument for just this purpose.

There are many accounts of the practice of "dancing the slaves," some from as early as the 1690s. The recollection of Alexander Falconbridge, a surgeon on a slave ship in the late 1700s, is one of the more sympathetic. He wrote in his 1788 book *An Account of the Slave Trade on the Coast of Africa,*

Exercise being deemed necessary for the preservation of their health, they are sometimes obliged to dance, when the weather will permit their coming on deck. If they go about it reluctantly, or do not move with agility, they are flogged; a person standing by them all the time with a cat-o-nine-tails in his hand for that purpose. Their music, upon these occasions, consists of a drum. . . . The poor wretches are frequently compelled to sing also; but when they do so, their songs are generally, as may naturally be expected, melancholy lamentations of their exile from their native country.

How sad it must have made these enslaved people to be forced to dance on the decks of the slave ships. In their native cultures, dancing was a joyous expression of

4

freedom. Music and dance had been an integral part of life back in Africa, associated with religion, with farming, with births and deaths, and weddings and other ceremonies. It had been a way to bring the members of a community together. Now, they were being forced to dance to survive, and to make the slave traders rich.

But dance would not only help the slaves to survive in a physical sense in the New World. It would also help them to stay alive in spirit, and that was something that slave masters could not take away from them. And because enslaved Africans brought their dances to the New World, over time their dances, like their music, would have a profound effect on the cultures there.

Once they arrived in the New World, the slaves in different areas found widely varied reactions to their singing and dancing. In the West Indies and the Caribbean, where the Catholic countries of France and Spain had established colonies, slaves were allowed to retain many elements of their own cultures. Serious attempts were made to Christianize them, for they were considered souls to be saved.

The slaves found much to identify with in the large numbers of saints worshipped in the Catholic faith. These saints seemed much like their own gods. In fact, slaves who converted to Catholicism often worshipped their favorite African gods right along with the Catholic saints. They also were allowed to worship in their own fashion, which meant lots of singing and dancing. The dances of religious cults like Santeria in Brazil, Shango in Trinidad, and Vaudou (Voodoo) in Haiti were, and still are, very

similar to the religious dances of the Yoruba peoples of Nigeria, from which many of the slaves came.

Slave dancing that had nothing to do with religion also flourished in the West Indies. Some of the most popular dances were competitive dances called Juba or Jumba, based on an African step dance called Giouba, a kind of elaborate jig. In these, dancers would challenge one another with their skill and agility, and the one who could outdance and outlast the rest was the winner.

There were also dances that were specific to certain holidays or occasions. In Trinidad, at Christmastime, the slaves were usually given a three-day holiday, and they danced throughout the three days. Many of the dances were ring dances, in which the slaves danced in a circle, always counterclockwise, and without lifting their feet from the ground. Other holidays marked by dance included the Carnival or Mardi Gras before Lent.

There were wedding dances, which were not all that common because only a few favored slaves who worked in their masters' houses had elaborate weddings, which were paid for by their masters. More common were funeral dances. The enslaved Africans carried on in the New World the worship of a god of cemeteries, called Gède. At funerals, Gède did a special dance called the Banda. Gède was also the god of reproduction, and his dance symbolized death and life, as well as the celebration of the future and the past in the present moment.

Then there were "crop-over" dances to celebrate the harvest. Sometimes the masters joined in these dances, because they, too, were happy that the crop was in.

While they retained their own traditional dances, en-slaved Africans in the West Indies and other areas in the Southern Hemisphere of the New World also adopted some of the dances of their masters. Oddly enough, one of the best examples of this adoption can be found among the Maroons of Jamaica. Around 1690, when the island was under Spanish rule, a group of slaves revolted against their masters and escaped to the mountainous regions of the island. They lived as free men, and so did their descen-dants. Yet the black dancer and sociologist Katherine Dunham, who lived among the Maroons for a time in the 1930s, noted that they danced many of the formal dances of the whites of two and half centuries earlier.

Blacks in Jamaica who remained enslaved also adopted white music and dance customs. In 1825, Alexander Bar-clay wrote about a crop-over dance: "About twenty years ago, it was common on occasions of this kind, to see the different African tribes forming each a distinct party, sing-ing and dancing to the *gumbay*, after the rude manners of their native Africa; but this custom is now extinct. Fol-lowing the example of the white people, the fiddle, which they play pretty well, is now the leading instrument; they dance Scotch reels. . . ." It is unlikely that Barclay knew what kind of dancing the slaves did when they were by themselves, and it is equally unlikely that traditional Afri-can dances had completely died out among them.

In the Northern Hemisphere, enslaved Africans had a different experience. For one thing, the predominantly Protestant English colonists in North America did not gen-

erally regard them as human—they considered slaves to be property, like horses and farm equipment. They did not worry about their souls. There were serious attempts on the part of some to convert the slaves to Christianity, but those who sought to convert them required that they give up all of their "heathen" beliefs and practices. There was no room in the Protestant faith for saints and lesser gods, and not much room for religious dancing either, for dancing was regarded as sinful by many Protestant sects. All of this was very hard for the African slaves to accept, for in their culture dance was a means of establishing contact with their ancestors and with the gods.

But in some areas the ring dance became a part of slave worship in the Protestant church. One group of worshippers would sing a spiritual in rhythm while another group would shuffle counterclockwise in single file around the church. If a dancer started to lift his or her feet, a watchful deacon would warn, "Look out, Sister (or Brother), how you walk on the Cross, your foot might slip and your soul get lost." There was a great variety of dance that could be accomplished without lifting the feet—shuffles, weight shifts, bending and shifting the knees, rotating, bending, and shifting the body.

There were far more opportunities to dance on the plantations than in church. This was especially true on big plantations where the slaves were left largely to themselves. It was not unusual for a group of slaves to go into the woods at night so they could dance without worrying about being observed. These dances were often the same dances that the slaves remembered having done in Africa.

At other times, the slaves simply danced in the slave quarters. They usually had Sunday off, and so Saturday night was a time of celebration, with much singing and dancing. The favored musical instrument to accompany dancing was the drum, which the slaves made from hollowed-out logs or nail kegs, with animal skins stretched tightly over one end. Much like the drums in Africa, these drums were used not only to make music but also to communicate. For some time, slave masters did not know that the slaves were using drumbeats as a sort of "Morse code" to send messages from one plantation to another. But after a series of revolts in the 1730s and 1740s, whites began to realize that the drums were not just innocent musical instruments. For example, in 1739, on a plantation called Stono about twenty miles west of Charleston, South Carolina, a group of slaves led by a slave named Cato killed two guards in a warehouse and stole arms and ammunition. Then they set off for Florida, beating two drums and calling to slaves on the plantations they passed to join them. More slaves did join them, and they managed to fight off or kill every white who tried to stop them.

Whites had already suspected that the drums were used by the slaves to "talk" to one another. A slave informer may well have told his master about this unique form of communication. But after the Stono insurrectionists marched to the sounds of drums, the Slave Codes of 1740 were passed. Large drums were banned entirely.

Slaves were forced to turn to other instruments to provide rhythm for their dancing and singing. They stretched cow hides over cheese boxes and made tambourines. They took cow bones and dried them in the sun, and used

9

them as a percussion instrument. And, lacking instruments of any kind, they always had their feet, as well as their bodies. For example, in one dance, called "Pattin' Juba," the side of the thigh and the hip was patted and clapped in a syncopated rhythm.

Back in Africa, some tribes had used their heels to tap out rhythms on sun-baked clay. In the New World, slaves did the same thing on the floors of their huts or the boards of their dancing floors. As recently as 1942, a white folklorist named Lydia Parrish found blacks in McIntosh County, Georgia, making drum sounds with their feet: "It always rouses my admiration to see the way in which the McIntosh County 'shouters' tap their heels on the resonant board floor to imitate the beat of the drum their forbears were not allowed to have. Those who hear the records of the musical chants which accompany the ring-shout . . . cannot believe that a drum is not used, though how the effect is achieved with the heels alone—when they barely leave the floor—remains a puzzle."

Parrish referred to the dance as a "ring-shout," and that term is commonly used. But no one is sure where the name came from. Because some slaves from Africa had come into contact with Moslem Arabs, some scholars have suggested that the word *shout* was originally the Arabic word *saut*, which meant "to run or walk around the Kaaba," the holy Moslem shrine in Mecca. And, like the slaves, Moslems always circle the Kaaba in a counter-clockwise direction. Others suggest simply that the slaves shouted as they danced.

As in the West Indies, harvesttime in North America was always a big occasion and involved much dancing.

In fact, some of the best dancing took place at harvesttime, because of the importance of the occasion. Some slaves, dressed in their best clothes and carrying candles or burning pine knots, would form a circle. Others inside the circle would dance using the motions of work, described by one writer this way: "swinging a scythe, tossing a pitchfork of hay into a wagon, hoisting a cotton-bale, rolling a hogshead of tobacco, sawing wood, hoeing corn—without the restriction and effort imposed by the load."

It was at harvest festivals that the Cakewalk developed. By some accounts, it was once called the "chalk-line walk," and it was a dance done by couples along a straight path, balancing buckets of water on their heads. Later on, it came to be called the Cakewalk because the winning couple would be presented with a cake, often something as simple as a corn cake. It was an elaborate and festive dance, and couples dressed in their best clothes (although it was not until much later, after slavery was abolished, that blacks would have had the fine clothes worn in the Cakewalk picture shown in this book, which is dated in the 1890s and is in the collection of the Museum of Modern Art). Dances that involved balancing buckets or glasses of water on the head were common among the slaves, and related directly to the African custom of carrying bundles and buckets and baskets on the head.

There were Christmas dances, Saturday-night dances, corn-shucking and quilting dances, wedding and funeral dances. In early years, funeral dances on plantations in the southern part of North America were very similar to those in the West Indies. These dances survived a long time in places like the Sea Islands off the coasts of Georgia

11

and South Carolina, where escaped slaves sought refuge and carried on their traditions without the interference or influence of whites. Funeral dances usually involved a march to the cemetery accompanied by drums, and a circular dance around the grave, either to keep away unwelcome spirit visitors or to keep "in" the spirit of the dead person.

Traditional African animal dances also found expression in the slave dances of North America. One was called the Buzzard Lope, another the Turkey Trot, and another the Snake Hips. There were also the Mosquito Dance, the Fish Tail, and the Camel Walk. In each, the dancer imitated the animal, bird, reptile, or insect in question.

Many of these African dances were kept alive for so long because of the constant influx of new slaves from Africa, or from Africa via the West Indies. They arrived with fresh memories of the homeland and helped older slaves, and even slaves who had never known Africa, to keep the traditions alive.

Of great influence on North American slave culture were the blacks who arrived in Louisiana from Santo Domingo after that island was taken over by former slaves and renamed Haiti in 1804. As a result of the Haitian Revolution, Haitian slaves gained their freedom, never to lose it again. This was more than half a century before freedom came to American blacks. Haitian blacks remained isolated from the white-ruled countries that surrounded them and thus were able to retain more of African culture than were blacks in white-dominated countries.

Many of Haiti's French colonials escaped to Louisiana. Louisiana contained the closest French culture, and had

only recently (1803) been purchased from France by the United States. These French colonists took with them as many slaves as they could. A number of free blacks from Santo Domingo also sought refuge in Louisiana, for they identified more with the French than with the slave revolutionaries. Together, these blacks, slave and free, had a great effect on the culture of Louisiana, particularly of New Orleans, where the majority settled. They brought with them Vaudou (Voodoo) as well as the weekly dances in Congo Square that many whites came to watch.

Slave importation was outlawed in the United States at just about the time the refugees from Haiti were arriving in Louisiana, but it was carried on illegally for some time afterward. Slaves continued to be brought to the States from the West Indies, and slaves were still traded within the states. Each new arrival contributed in some way to maintaining the tradition of African dancing in North America, and by the early 1800s, blacks were not the only ones to engage in the African-influenced dances.

From the very beginning, the dances of the slaves interested and intrigued their white masters, and before long slave dances were being used as a form of entertainment for whites. When the master had a party, he would summon the most talented dancers from the slave quarters and have them dance for his guests. At other times, he might take his guests to the slave quarters on a Saturday night to watch the slaves dancing for themselves. Black musicians frequently played at white dances, and even though they usually played "white" instruments like the fiddle, their special rhythms influenced the way the whites danced. In Virginia, around the time of the American Revo-

lution, it was a popular custom for whites at their cotillions (formal ballroom dances) to close the evening with a slave-style "Negro jig."

Sometimes, whites danced right along with the slaves. Isaac Jefferson, a slave at Thomas Jefferson's plantation at Monticello, reported that Thomas' brother, Randolph Jefferson, "used to come out among black people, play the fiddle and dance half the night."

Especially at harvesttime, some whites would join the slaves in celebrating the crop. Of course, the whites had more reason to celebrate than the slaves, since the whites were the ones who stood to benefit from a good harvest. Thus, it was very early that African dances began to influence white dancing and that black dance began to be a part of American culture.

From "jazz dancing" to "break dancing," modern dance is heavily influenced by African dance forms. At the same time, many of today's black dancers are stars in traditional white forms of dance, like ballet, although their success in this area has been especially hard-won. This is the story of black dance in America, told through the lives of the people whose innovations in dance influenced the majority culture. It is also the story of the people who pioneered the efforts to prove to whites that blacks could excel in "white" dance styles.

Chapter 2
From Minstrelsy to the Follies

Even before the American Revolutionary War, white entertainers were doing slave-style dances onstage. One of the first was an actor named Tea who appeared with The American Company in Philadelphia in 1767 and performed a "Negro Dance." To appear more authentic, he blackened his face with burnt cork. Other actors copied him, and their performances planted the seeds of the minstrel shows that would become popular in the late 1820s.

Minstrel shows depended almost entirely on black dance, music, and dialect. They were also performed almost exclusively by white entertainers. Minstrelsy is said to have started with Thomas Rice, a white actor who happened to see an old black man singing and dancing in the stable behind the theater where Rice was performing. The old man had a crooked look to him: One shoulder

15

was higher than the other, and one leg twisted at the knee. So, when he danced a jig, it was with a limp that Rice thought uproariously funny. He learned that the old man called himself Daddy Jim Crow—Daddy, because that's what old black men were frequently called, and Jim Crow after his master. Soon afterward, Thomas Rice had changed his name to Daddy "Jim Crow" Rice and had built an entire blackface act around an imitation of the old man's crooked jig. The act caused a sensation, and within months there were dozens of white entertainers doing similar acts. By the 1840s, there were entire shows in which actors in blackface performed skits, songs, and dances.

The format of the shows was based on black dance, especially circle and hand-clapping dances. In a minstrel show, the entertainers sat in chairs arranged in a semicircle on the stage. In minstrelsy, the master of ceremonies was called the interlocutor. Those who sang the melody for the dance were the chorus, clapping their hands or shaking tambourines. Every man in the chorus had the chance to do a solo bit of some sort, just as blacks had in many African dance ceremonies.

Almost all these bits parodied blacks, and it was the minstrel shows that established some of the stereotypes of blacks that exist even today—the grinning, shuffling, dumb Negro; the citified dandy; the watermelon eater. Because of these negative associations, "Jim Crow" later came to refer to the racist segregation laws that were passed at the end of the nineteenth century.

Most blacks, meanwhile, could not get on a white stage, no matter how talented they were. Occasionally, a master

would sponsor one of his slaves who showed musical or dancing talent. But this was rare. Rare, too, were the free blacks who managed to be successful on white stages. But there was one, Juba, who created a sensation on his own, in the middle of the nineteenth century.

Juba
(William Henry Lane)

Very little is known about the early years of this talented dancer. Few records were kept on blacks unless they happened to be someone's property, and it is likely that Lane was born free around 1825, somewhere east of the Mississippi. Lane probably learned much of his dancing from "Uncle" Jim Lowe, a jig and reel dancer who, because he was black, performed in saloons and dance halls, rather than on the stages of regular theaters.

By the early 1840s, Lane had so distinguished himself that he was appearing frequently on New York stages. He called himself Master Juba, after the competitive dancing style he favored, and which derived from the African step dance called Giouba. By most accounts, the dancing he did was not distinctly African in origin but rather a combination of an Irish jig and African steps like the shuffle and the slide, together with upper body movements that were also African in origin (in European dances like the jig, the upper body does not move).

Whatever his style, Juba did what talented black dancers had always done, and that was to include in the dances he did a style that was all his own—with syncopation,

improvisation, and an emphasis on rhythm and percussion (rather than melody) that would later be the basis of tap dancing. He was judged to be one of the best dancers in the country, black or white. This didn't sit well with Master John Diamond, a white dancer who had made a name for himself dancing jigs in blackface. In 1844, Diamond challenged Juba to a series of dancing contests. The first one, held at John Tryon's Amphitheatre in New York City, was a draw—both men danced so well that neither was the clear winner. But after two more matches, at the Chatham and Bowery Theaters in New York, Juba had won the title "King of All Dancers."

In 1845, Juba toured with three white men who called themselves the Georgia Champion Minstrels. Blacks were rarely allowed on white stages alone, much less in integrated company. Moreover, he received top billing on the program at the theaters where he performed. The following year, he performed with (Charles) White's Ethiopian Serenaders at White's Melodeon in New York.

He also toured New England with the Georgia Champion Minstrels. Handbills for the show advertised him as: "The Wonder of the World, Juba, Acknowledged to be the Greatest Dancer in the World. Having danced at the Chatham Theatre for $500, and at the Bowery Theatre for the same amount, and established himself as King of All Dancers. No conception can be formed of the variety of beautiful and intricate steps exhibited by him with ease. You must see to believe."

In 1848, Juba traveled to London with (Gilbert Ward) Pell's Ethiopian Serenaders to perform at Vauxhall Gardens

18

in June. One reviewer wrote, "The dancing of Juba exceeded anything ever witnessed in Europe. The style as well as the execution is unlike anything ever seen in this country. The manner in which he beats time with his feet, and the extraordinary command he possesses over them, can only be believed by those who have been present at his exhibition." And another wrote, "The performances of this young man are far above the common performances of the mountebanks who give imitations of American and Negro characters."

Juba and Pell's Ethiopian Serenaders were so popular in London that they were booked solidly into 1851. After an engagement at Cremorne Gardens that year, the Serenaders apparently returned to the United States. Juba, who had married an English girl, remained. Sadly, he died in 1852, when he was only about twenty-seven years old, and thus never had the chance to influence American dancing as much as he might have. Some scholars feel, however, that it was due to Juba that the dancing in minstrel shows retained more integrity as a black art form than the songs or skits.

Minstrelsy as a true imitation of black culture grew very stale very quickly. Part of the reason was that it was difficult for the white entertainers to get fresh material because they had to hang around blacks more than they wished to in order to hear their jokes, pick up their speech patterns, and even listen to their songs. But it was fairly easy to observe authentic Negro dancing, not only on the plantations but also in public places like saloons and dance halls.

19

However, by this time minstrel dancers could not go to Congo Square in New Orleans for their research, for the dancing in Congo Square had been suppressed in the 1840s. Of course, there never was anything very authentically black about minstrelsy, at least not as long as blacks were barred from it.

By the time slavery was abolished and blacks were allowed into minstrel shows, true minstrelsy was past its heyday. Its rules were so set that even blacks had to put on blackface to be judged real minstrels! But the entrance of blacks onto the minstrelsy stage probably accounted more than anything else for its continued survival into the twentieth century, when it became part of vaudeville, medicine shows, fairs, carnivals, tent shows, and fraternity shows even into the 1950s. One of the most successful of the black minstrel companies was the Georgia Minstrels, organized by Charles Hicks in 1865. Others in the boom days of black minstrelsy were the Hicks and Sawyer Minstrels, Richards' and Pringle's Minstrels, and the McCabe and Young Minstrels.

Few blacks successful in minstrelsy made their fame only as dancers. Most were of necessity comedians and musicians as well. Billy Kersands, for example, was a superb dancer, but he was probably more famous for his comedy routines. The Bohee Brothers did dance duets, but they were more famous for the duets they played on their banjos. Even Juba played the tambourine.

However, it didn't take black minstrels long to realize that whites were keenly interested in black dancing, and most of the black minstrel shows featured more dancing

20

than the white minstrel shows did. But it was a team of black entertainers who had the idea of exploiting the African roots of black dance. Bert Williams and George Walker are remembered best as a musical-comedy team, but in dance history they are credited with helping black dance to really flourish at the close of the nineteenth century.

Williams and Walker

Egbert Williams was born in the Bahamas in 1876, but grew up in Riverside, California. He was studying civil engineering in San Francisco when he decided to become an entertainer. George Walker was born in Lawrence, Kansas, but left town as a young man to follow a group of black minstrels. He ended up in San Francisco in 1893, where he met Bert Williams and persuaded Williams to form a musical comedy act with him. The two decided that since white men were so successful pretending to be "coons," which was an unflattering racial nickname, they ought to be able to do well by billing themselves as the "Two Real Coons."

They got their chance sooner than they had expected. That year, at the Mid-Winter Fair in San Francisco, the managers of the fair had decided to feature native dancers from Dahomey, in West Africa. Unfortunately, the dancers were delayed in sailing for San Francisco, and at the last minute the fair directors were forced to search for a replacement. Then it dawned on them that fair-goers would not know real Africans from fake ones. So they put out a

call for local black dancers to appear as the Dahomeyans. Bert Williams and George Walker were among those who answered the call.

Neither Williams nor Walker, nor any of the others, were exactly sure how Dahomeyans danced, so they moved about in as primitive a manner as possible, stepping wildly to the beat of jungle drums. When the real Dahomeyans arrived, Williams and Walker were out of a job, but by this time they were intrigued with the idea of real African dancing, and they studied the authentic dances intently. They also experienced the reaction of the crowds to the rhythmic excitement of African dancing. They realized that exotic African entertainment could be very popular.

Walker wrote in *Theatre* magazine in 1906 that he and Williams "were not long in deciding that if we ever reached the point of having a show of our own, we would delineate and feature African characters as far as we could and still remain American, and make our acting interesting and entertaining to American audiences."

In the meantime, however, they made fashionable a dance that was based on African dancing, although it is not certain that they were aware of its roots. It was the Cakewalk, the dance that slaves had first done on the plantations a couple of centuries earlier. Over the years, the Cakewalk had enjoyed ups and downs in popularity among whites. At one time in the South, it was popular among plantation owners and other upper-class whites, but that ended with the Civil War and the emancipation of the slaves. Former masters hardly wanted to be re-

22

minded of the good old days that were gone forever. By the later years of the nineteenth century, the Cakewalk had become popular among lower- and middle-class urban whites who went to bars and saloons where the syncopated jazz music called ragtime was played. But it was not a dance for "high society." Williams and Walker helped make it socially acceptable.

They had arrived in New York to appear in a show that, unfortunately, closed quickly. But the show had played long enough to persuade Koster and Bials, managers of a popular theater, to hire them. They were so well received that they played a record run of twenty-eight weeks. It was during this time that they first performed the Cakewalk, which the audiences loved. They decided to capitalize on their success and to get some publicity, by challenging William K. Vanderbilt, the most prominent millionaire in New York at that time, to a Cakewalk contest.

In January 1898, they delivered a written challenge to the Vanderbilt mansion. Vanderbilt never responded, but the newspapers thought it was a great story, and Williams and Walker got the publicity they sought. Pretty soon, a Cakewalk craze swept theaters and dance halls across the nation. It even inspired black composer Will Marion Cook and lyricist Paul Lawrence Dunbar to write an all-black musical titled *Clorindy—The Origin of the Cakewalk* especially for Williams and Walker. Unfortunately, by the time Cook and Dunbar managed to find a theater in which to present it, Williams and Walker were out of town, and Cook had to find other stars for his musical.

The team then went to London to try to launch them-

Bert Williams and George Walker, shown here with George's wife, Ada Overton Walker, in *In Dahomey* (1903), were the first black entertainment team to use African themes in their shows. *Theatre and Music Collection, Museum of the City of New York.*

24

selves and the Cakewalk there, and through their efforts, the Cakewalk became the first black-based fad dance to become popular in both America and Europe. Had their reception in London been more enthusiastic, Williams and Walker might have continued primarily as dancers. But the British apparently liked the Cakewalk more than they liked Williams and Walker. The team returned to the States and turned to musical comedy. By 1902, they were producing shows with African settings and songs with African names, but dance was not a major part of these shows.

Williams and Walker went on to become popular musical comedy stars. Their first musical play, *In Dahomey*, was also the first black show ever to open on Broadway. Unfortunately, George Walker fell ill in 1908 and never performed on a stage again. Bert Williams went on to become the first black performer with the Ziegfeld Follies, although he was not allowed to ride the passenger elevator in the theater—as a black man, he was forced to ride the freight elevator. Between 1913 and 1917, he was the *only* black performer on Broadway, and although it was hard for him to be in that unique position, he stuck with it, explaining, "We've got our foot in the door, we mustn't let it close again." He, too, died young, of pneumonia at the age of forty-six.

In black dance history, and in black cultural history generally, Williams and Walker made their biggest contributions during their early careers. It was then that they challenged racial stereotypes and made an effort to bring some fresh material and approaches to their performances. They introduced African characters such as kings and pow-

erful warriors into their shows and were able to demonstrate to white audiences that not all blacks could be stereotyped as stock minstrel characters. And, most significantly in the history of black dance, they helped pave the way for the first appearance of a black movement in ballroom dancing by making the Cakewalk fashionable.

There was no real tradition of ballroom dancing among black Americans, for the obvious reason that most of them couldn't afford to go to ballrooms even if they could be admitted. Ballroom dancing also was more often taught by instructors than learned by observation, and that, too, made it difficult for blacks to participate. Black social dances did exist and were done in dance halls and honky-tonks throughout the South, but whites knew little about these dances. Whites tended to associate black dancing with low-life dancing, the kind found in saloons, not in ballrooms. In this way, black dancing was much like black music. In the eyes of most whites, if it was black, it was low-class.

That was how ragtime music was regarded at the turn of the century, although it would later become acceptable to whites. The low esteem with which ragtime music was regarded bothered the ragtime composer Scott Joplin. He believed that ragtime was just as complex as European classical music, and he worked hard to make ragtime music respectable. In the closing years of the century, he composed a dramatic ragtime folk ballet called *The Ragtime Dance*. It consisted of a vocal introduction followed by a series of dance themes directed by the vocalist and based on black social dances of the era: Ragtime Dance, Clean-

Up Dance, Jennie Cooks Dance, Slow Drag, World's Fair Dance, Back Step Prance, Dude Walk, Sedidus Walk, Town Talk, and Stop Time. So convinced was Joplin that the composition would be popular if someone would only publish it that he used his own money to form The Scott Joplin Drama Company and to stage, in late 1899, a single performance of the folk ballet in Sedalia, Missouri. But that was the only performance ever staged. No music publishing company would publish the ballet, and his hopes for its success were dashed.

More successful in the area of ballroom dancing were Dora Dean and Charles Johnson. They had achieved their first success dancing the Cakewalk ten years before the one and only performance of Scott Joplin's ill-fated *The Ragtime Dance*. Although they would develop an elegant image, they remained in the mainstream of popular dance and so were not criticized for being pretentious as, unfortunately, Joplin was criticized.

Dora Dean

Nine years before Williams and Walker made their splash in New York with the Cakewalk, Dora Dean and Charles Johnson were strutting in the Cakewalk finale of an all-black show called *The Creole Show* in New York. Both were solo dancers at the time. Johnson was an "eccentric dancer," and Dean billed herself simply as a dancer. Johnson had first learned of the Cakewalk from his mother, an ex-slave, who remembered the Cakewalks on the Missouri plantation where she had been born. Back in those

days, it had been done by individuals. *The Creole Show* was a departure from the norm in minstrelsy because women were included for the first time, and this permitted more variations in the dancing. As a couple, Johnson and Dean did such a magnificent version of the Cakewalk that they established a place for themselves as a cakewalking act.

Of the two, Dora Dean was the more famous. Born Dora Babbige in Covington, Kentucky, around 1872, she probably had little formal training before she made her first hit in *The Creole Show*, which premiered in Boston in 1899. She did an exhibition Cakewalk and became so well known for it that she was able to get solo engagements at vaudeville theaters and roof gardens in New York and elsewhere in the Northeast.

She was a beautiful woman, and she inspired Bert Williams, for one, to compose a song to "Miss Dora Dean":

> *Oh, have you ever seen Miss Dora Dean,*
> *She is the sweetest gal you ever seen.*
> *Some day I'm going to make this Gal my Queen.*
> *On next Sunday morning, I'm going to marry*
> *Miss Dora Dean.*

Williams and Walker sang the song in their New York debut, and no doubt it contributed to their success.

Unfortunately for Williams, he never got the chance to marry the beautiful Dora Dean, who married her dancing partner, Charles Johnson. The two had an outstanding engagement at the Madison Square Garden roof theater in 1895 and became favorites on the vaudeville circuit.

Originating on plantations as a festival dance—at "crop-over" time, or harvesttime—the Cakewalk became a national dance craze in the 1890s. Bert Williams and George Walker even challenged the white millionaire William K. Vanderbilt to a Cakewalk contest. *Collection, The Museum of Modern Art, New York.*

Their act was marked by the elegance of their costuming and of their bearing. Dora Dean was the first black entertainer to wear thousand-dollar costumes. As a dancing duo, they were the first successful blacks in ballroom dancing, and certainly the most elegant and sophisticated. They were also among the few blacks to break into white vaudeville in the early years of the twentieth century. They toured Europe and in fact spent more time there than in the United States in the early 1900s.

After her marriage and dancing partnership with Charles Johnson broke up after 1914, Dora Dean returned to the United States. For several years, she had successful engagements in vaudeville with shows entitled *Dora Dean & Co.* and *Dora Dean and Her Phantoms*. Some of these shows featured the white child performers Seymour Felix and Amalia Caire, whose act was called Felix and Caire. Dean retired in the 1920s, but she and her ex-husband and partner Charles Johnson had a "reunion" booking at the Harlem nightclub Connie's Inn in 1936. She died in January 1950 in Minneapolis, Minnesota.

There is only one recorded example of a black doing a solo classical dance in those early years of the twentieth century. Ada Overton Walker, George Walker's wife, who starred in many of the Williams and Walker shows, so impressed William Hammerstein that he invited her to do a solo interpretation of *Salome*. The famous white dancers Gertrude Hoffman and Ruth St. Denis had already danced *Salome*, but no black dancer had ever done so. Hammerstein was one of the few white producers who would not be dissuaded by considerations of race. Report-

edly, Ada Walker did well, but no successful career in serious dance followed.

Even the classiest, most impressive black acts had trouble gaining acceptance in most white theaters in the early years of the twentieth century. Only in the big northern cities were there large enough black populations to support black theaters for shows or vaudeville acts. Only in the big northern cities were whites sophisticated enough to occasionally allow black performers on their stages. And attitudes were constantly changing with political and social events. In New York, for example, blacks enjoyed some success at downtown theaters and on Broadway in the first decade of the century. But after the black heavyweight boxer Jack Johnson beat the white fighter Jim Jeffries in 1910, there were anti-black riots in the city, and many blacks began moving northward to Harlem to escape. As mentioned earlier, between 1913 and 1917, Bert Williams was the only black performer on Broadway, and he was forced to perform the caricatures that whites expected of him.

Talented blacks in the new black community of Harlem formed their own theater and music companies. While there were no dance companies per se, a company like the Lafayette Theater Stock Players relied heavily on dancing in its shows, and its most successful show ever—*The Darktown Follies*—was filled with dancing.

The Darktown Follies

Written and staged by J. Leubrie Hill, an ex-member of the Williams and Walker company, *The Darktown Follies*

31

was produced in 1913, about a year after the Lafayette Theater opened at 2227 Seventh Avenue (corner of 131st Street) in Harlem. Originally, the theater had been built for whites, with a segregated seating area for blacks, but by this time more and more blacks were moving uptown to Harlem, and the owners were forced to close the theater. It was then leased by Lester Walton, a drama critic for the black newspaper *New York Age*. He hired a stock company and set about offering a variety of entertainment, from grand opera to Shakespearean plays to black versions of popular Broadway shows. *The Darktown Follies* was the company's first venture into original black musical comedy.

The show was heavy on dance and was one of the first to feature tap dancing. Tap dancing was a relatively new form, but one that could be traced back to the early slave dances in which the dancers used their feet to make rhythmic sounds on floorboards or hard-packed earth. During the minstrelsy era, this kind of dancing was blended with Irish jig dancing, where the whole emphasis was on the movement of the legs and feet, not of the upper body. Juba became famous for his syncopated, percussive dancing. This type of dance became known as the Clog. By the late years of the nineteenth century, some dancers were investing the Clog with more of the upper-body movements of dances like the Pigeon Wing. A new dance style, called the Buck and Wing, was first introduced on the New York stage by a dancer named James McIntyre. The Buck was close to a Time Step, and the Wing was a hop with one foot flung out to the side. Soon, almost every kind of dance that featured rhythmic or syncopated

foot movements together with upper-body movements was called a Buck and Wing dance. Many dance historians believe that there is a close connection between this type of dancing and ragtime music. By the turn of the century, Buck and Wing dancing was being called simply Tap.

Toots Davis and Eddie Rector did tap dancing in *The Darktown Follies*. Ethel Williams and others in the company performed a dance called the Texas Tommy, done by couples, which featured two basic steps, a kick and a hop three times on each foot, followed by whatever the dancers felt like doing. There was even a Cakewalk finale. But the most popular number was the finale of the first act, titled "At the Ball," which featured a dance that became another black dance craze: "Ballin' the Jack."

It was a circular dance, and thus related to the ring-shout. The dancers' heads and shoulders remained still, and the primary movement was in the torso, an undulating, hip-rotating series of movements. The dancers accompanied themselves with hand-clapping. It was a dance that had been around for some time, but it was the staging in *The Darktown Follies* that made it so exciting. The writer James Weldon Johnson remembered, "The whole company formed an endless chain that passed before the footlights and behind the scenes, round and round, singing and executing a movement from a dance called 'ballin' the jack,' one of those Negro dances that periodically sweep the country." They danced with such exuberance that only the most nonrhythmic member of the audience could resist moving his body and tapping his feet and clapping his hands right along with them.

Within days of the premiere of *The Darktown Follies*,

the "At the Ball" number was the talk of Harlem, and very shortly, it was the talk of all New York. Johnson wrote that it was the subject of headlines and even cartoons in the downtown New York papers. Carl Van Vechten, who had been music critic for *The New York Times* and was at the time that paper's Paris correspondent, wrote that the dancers "grew mad with their bodies," and so naturally this was something that white downtowners wanted to see. According to James Weldon Johnson, it was at this time that Harlem's reputation as an exciting nightspot began and that it became fashionable to go to Harlem in search of entertainment.

Florenz Ziegfeld, the owner of the Ziegfeld Follies, the most popular white downtown show at the time, was not content to leave "At the Ball" in Harlem. He purchased rights to the act for inclusion in his own show, and it was one of the greatest hits the Follies ever had.

Two years later, in 1915, the Lafayette Theater tried to repeat the success of *The Darktown Follies* with a similar show called *Darkydom*. It had music by Will Marion Cook and starred a popular comedy team called Miller and Lyles, but it failed to include any exciting dance pieces and was not particularly successful.

Not until 1921 would another black musical excite the general public with its dancing. By then, World War I had ended, and the victorious U.S. troops had come home (the members of the all-black New York regiment, nick-named the "hell-fighters" for their bravery in the European trenches, were treated to a parade up Fifth Avenue). The war had had a profound effect on the nation. It had been

34

the first war to truly affect the entire world, and in a sense, the nation had lost its innocence; no longer did people have absolute faith in humankind. Many Americans began to view the future less optimistically and to take pride in a worldly cynicism, while at the same time mourning the passing of a more simple time.

For most Americans, the vague sense of unrest never reached conscious expression. But there was a sense of change and upheaval. Women, as well as blacks, had enjoyed unprecedented opportunities in the workplace during the war; soon these women would cut their hair and shorten their skirts and demand greater freedom as well as the right to vote. In 1919, the year after the war ended, Congress passed the Volstead Act, outlawing the manufacture and sale of liquor and opening the way for organized crime to make millions in the bootleg-liquor trade. This only made more Americans want to drink, and the nightlife of most big cities flourished, rather than suffered, as a result. Added to all this was the prosperity of the postwar period. It was an era ripe for major social upheaval.

Shuffle Along

Against this backdrop, the first black show since 1908 opened on Broadway. *Shuffle Along* was the creation of two black musical comedy teams, Sissle and Blake and Miller and Lyles. Noble Sissle and Eubie Blake had been successful on the white vaudeville circuits, as had Flournoy Miller and Aubrey Lyles. But all four bemoaned the condi-

Shuffle Along (1921), the first all-black show on Broadway, started the Harlem Renaissance of the 1920s and spawned a host of imitations. It was created by two black comedy teams who wrote, directed, and starred in the show. From left, Noble Sissle, Eubie Blake, Flournoy Miller, and Aubrey Lyles. *Performing Arts Research Center, New York Public Library.*

tions of life on the road and the caricatures they were forced to play. They agreed that the only way to put black performers on a white stage with any dignity was through musical comedy, and decided to create their own show.

They did so on a shoestring, using cast-off costumes and sets. They wrote the show around these castoffs, and so in the same show they had a plantation scene and a Far Eastern scene. The plot line was thin, but the show had some excellent songs written by Sissle and Blake. Most important of all was the cast of energetic young singers and dancers who were so thrilled at the chance to perform.

Shuffle Along opened at the broken-down old 63rd Street Theater on May 22, 1921, to very little fanfare. Major critics didn't bother to attend the opening-night performance, but reviewers who did attend gave the show good reviews, which, in turn, interested the top critics. Very shortly after, *Shuffle Along* was getting rave reviews, and it became a smash hit.

What everyone raved about was the sheer energy of the show. Heywood Broun wrote in the *Evening World*, "No musical show in town boasts such rousing team-work. . . . We don't suppose the members of the cast and chorus actually pay for the privilege of appearing in the performance, but there is every indication that there is nothing in the world which they would rather do. They are all terribly glad to be up on the stage singing and dancing. Their training is professional, but the spirit is amateur. The combination is irresistible."

Critic Alan Dale of the New York *American* wrote: "At times it seemed as though nothing would stop the chorus

from singing and dancing except ringing down the curtain. They revelled in their work; they simply pulsed with it, and there was no let-up at all. And gradually any tired feeling that you might have been nursing vanished in the sun of their good humor and you didn't mind how long they 'shuffled along.' You even felt like shuffling a bit with them. All of which I admit isn't usual in dear old Forty-second street."

Elsewhere in the review, Dale described the show as full of "pep," and it was this energy to which audiences responded. The energy, and the wonderful music and dancing. The music was completely nontraditional, and was heavily weighted in favor of ragtime (sadly, Scott Joplin, who had died in 1917 impoverished and unhappy, did not live to see this elevation of his favorite music). The dancing was jazz dancing, including just about every current dance step, and heavy on tap, which *Shuffle Along* helped to legitimize.

Something else that *Shuffle Along* legitimized was the idea of romantic love between blacks. Many whites believed that black people were not capable of such "human" emotions and would have been upset with the idea that blacks could feel romantic love. In *Shuffle Along*, a black couple kissed onstage for the first time, during the number "Love Will Find a Way." Sissle and Blake and Miller and Lyles were so worried about the risk they were taking that they put the number just before the curtain came down at intermission, so they could make a quick exit if the white audience reacted with anger and violence. They were amazed when the audience instead called for an encore.

38

Shuffle Along played on Broadway for a full year, making stars of Florence Mills (who took over the female lead from Gertrude Saunders when Saunders left the show to go to Europe) and a gangly teenager named Josephine Baker, who would later become the toast of Europe. Among the replacement dancers was Elida Webb, who was to become an important choreographer. After it closed on Broadway, the show toured all over the country. Revivals of *Shuffle Along* were still enjoying great success into the 1930s. The show started a whole new era for blacks on Broadway, for it was followed by countless black musical revues. It is also credited with marking the start of the Harlem Renaissance, a period that lasted nearly a decade, when Harlem became a playground for whites and when black artists, writers, and entertainers enjoyed white critical and financial support such as had never been known before.

The most immediate effect of *Shuffle Along* was an absolute craze for jazz dancing. White New Yorkers suddenly decided that black dancing was not so low-life after all. In fact, judging by the young people in the show's chorus, this kind of dance seemed to be the ticket to happiness. Responding to this new interest, "colored dance studios" opened up, many on Broadway, to teach black dance styles like tap and the snakehips (first danced by plantation slaves) to eager whites. Among the most popular was Billy Pierce's studio. Pierce was white, but he hired black dancers to teach white stars like Ethel Barrymore. The director of Pierce's studio was the tap dancer Buddy Bradley, who created routines for many Broadway musicals

and later became popular in London as a choreographer for musicals, films, and ballets.

Whites who didn't feel like paying for lessons could get all the dance demonstrations they wanted at the big Harlem ballrooms such as the Savoy, the Renaissance, and the Alhambra. In response, the dancers there started putting on performances for the white "slummers." The writer Langston Hughes, who lived in Harlem at the time, recalled, "The lindy-hoppers at the Savoy even began to practice acrobatic routines, and to do absurd things for the entertainment of the whites, that probably never would have entered their heads to attempt merely for their own effortless amusement. Some of the lindy-hoppers had cards printed with their names on them and became dance professors teaching the tourists."

But the young black dancers at the Savoy ballroom and other dance halls in Harlem didn't need the stimulation of white audiences for their dance inventions and innovations. Dance was in the air in Harlem. The dancers in *Shuffle Along* had learned their steps not on stage but in local dance halls. The success of *Shuffle Along* served merely to publicize and popularize what had already been going on in Harlem.

Chapter 3
Jazz Dancing: The Harlem Renaissance of the 1920s

While black artists and writers enjoyed unprecedented attention from whites during the years of the Harlem Renaissance, 1921–1933, it was black musicians, singers, and dancers who really got the "rush" from whites in this period. Whites expected so-called "jungle rhythms" in music, exotic and acrobatic dancing, and songs with suggestive lyrics. So that is just what they were given, for blacks had never before enjoyed the opportunity to be seen and heard by such a large audience. Suddenly, black dancers had steady work, and they intended to keep working as long as they could.

For black dancers, there were jobs galore. Between 1921 and 1939, there were some forty black musicals, all with lots of dancing and with large chorus lines of dancers. It was these black shows that began the precision dancing (dancing in unison to a beat) that has been expected of

show chorus lines ever since. Then, too, there were all the jobs in the exclusive clubs that opened in Harlem, and elsewhere, such as the Cotton Club, Barron Wilkins' Exclusive Club, and Connie's Inn. The floor shows at these clubs were as lavish as anything seen on Broadway. The clubs catered to rich whites. In fact, many wouldn't allow black patrons in. But the waiters and entertainers were all black, and there were black dance choruses (the Cotton Club had "Cotton Club Girls" and "Cotton Club Boys") as well as individual black acts. The only barrier to working at these clubs was a dark complexion. Those who were hired, from waiters to chorus dancers, were uniformly light complected, as close to white as possible.

Dance craze after dance craze swept the country during this decade. Not for nothing was it called the "Roaring Twenties." The most famous dance was the Charleston, and there never was before, nor has been since, a craze quite like it.

The Charleston

Music scholars have traced the Charleston back to Africa, where similar movements were featured in the dances of the Ashanti people. In the 1940s, the dancer and anthropologist Katherine Dunham found Charleston steps done in Haiti. In the American South, it seems to be closest to a dance called the Jay-Bird. It is similar to the challenge dances, or Juba dances, of plantation days. Judging from its name, the version that arrived in New York came by way of Charleston, South Carolina.

It was first introduced in a black show called *Liza*, but it didn't become really popular until James Weldon Johnson wrote the hit song "Charleston" for the Miller and Lyles musical *Runnin' Wild* in 1923. Among the male chorus were the tap dancers Pete Nugent and Derby Wilson, who would later become well known, and future choreographer Sammy Dyer. Elida Webb, of *Shuffle Along* fame, staged all the musical and dance specialties and chorus numbers. As choreographed by Webb, the Charleston was very different from the slow Jay-Bird. This dance was fast. It was an exhibition dance that used the whole body in shimmying motions, included a fast kicking step, both forward and backward, and featured slapping the hands on the body, especially on the knees, while the dancers were in a knock-kneed position. This beating out of complex rhythms was something that most show-goers had never seen before, and the dance created a sensation.

The black dance studios couldn't satisfy the demand for Charleston lessons. According to an article in *The New York Times* on May 24, 1925, "Debutantes are practicing it at the Colony Club; society matrons are panting over it in Park Avenue boudoirs; department store clerks are trying to master it in the restrooms at the lunch hour; the models of the garment industry dance it together in the chop suey palaces at noontime; the flats of the West Side and the tenements of the East Side are not immune to the contagion." The article also stated, "Proprietors of employment agencies are being importuned to supply cooks, waitresses, laundresses and maids 'who can Charleston.'"

The image of a young white woman, wearing a short

By the 1920s, the chorus lines in black shows were doing jazz dancing.
Author's Collection.

"bob" haircut and an equally short fringed dress and dancing the Charleston, is the prevailing image of the Roaring Twenties. Such young women were called "flappers," probably because they flapped their arms and legs around like crazed birds when they did the dance.

It wasn't long before word of the new dance rage in the United States reached Europe, and more than one American black dancer went on to fame and fortune across the Atlantic because of the ability to dance the Charleston. One was Josephine Baker, who took Paris by storm in 1924 with her scanty costume and wild Charleston renditions. Another was Bricktop, born Ada Beatrice Queen Victoria Louise Virginia Smith, who became a celebrated Paris nightclub operator because she taught the British Duke of Windsor to do the Charleston.

The Black Bottom, a dance that was introduced in the 1924 show *Dinah*, became almost as popular as the Charleston. It, too, was based on black challenge dancing, and featured the slapping of the backside while hopping forward and backward. The version in *Dinah* came by way of Nashville, Tennessee. Later on, in the 1930s, there were new dance crazes, such as the Big Apple, the Suzy-Q, and Truckin'. But none of them ever topped the Charleston in popularity.

Elida Webb

Elida Webb claimed to have invented the Charleston. While there were many who disputed her, no one could argue with the fact that it was she who had choreographed

the dance in *Runnin' Wild* that gave rise to the Charleston craze. She was one of the first black choreographers for Broadway and had a hand in the careers of many black entertainers, dancers, singers, and actors.

Elida Webb was born in Alexandria, Virginia. Some sources give the year of her birth as 1896, others as 1898. Her father had once been servant to a man who had attended Dartmouth College, and family legend had it that Mr. Webb had studied there as well, although probably not as a formally enrolled student. He did pick up an education, however, and taught school in Virginia for a time. But teaching jobs were hard to come by. Elida was three when the family moved to New York City, where her father got a job as a waiter. Eventually, there were twelve children in the family. Elida was the only one who went into show business, against her father's wishes. However, she remained close to the family throughout her life and never learned to cook, relying on her sisters even when she was married.

Webb was very beautiful, and she moved with a natural grace. Ada Overton Walker discovered her when she was sixteen or seventeen and going to high school on Lenox Avenue and 134th Street. Walker invited Webb to join her stock company. Webb's father was against it, but her mother took her side. She joined Ada Walker's stock company as a dancer and studied the technique of the older woman as well as of the other dancers in the company. But she was a born leader and was soon choreographing dances for the group.

By 1912, she was staging shows at Reese and Webber,

46

the first nightclub on Broadway to offer floor shows. She also danced in shows when she couldn't get choreography work. While her personal life floundered—she married a musician and gambler named Majors, but they were divorced after he began to see another woman—her career as a dancer and choreographer flourished. She was hired to dance in *Shuffle Along* and was paid the same weekly salary ($30) as the other dancers, but she seems to have had more influence behind the scenes than the others did. Legend has it that it was she who discovered Josephine Baker in Philadelphia and later persuaded Sissle and Blake and Miller and Lyles to hire the teenager, whose cross-eyed antics in the chorus line added a new dimension to the show. Webb also got Fredi Washington a job with *Shuffle Along* and was thus credited with discovering the beautiful actress who would go on to major fame in plays and films. From *Shuffle Along*, Webb went to *Runnin' Wild*, where she really made her name as a choreographer.

In 1923, Webb got the chance to work as choreographer at the Cotton Club in Harlem and was one of the first blacks to break the "whites only" barrier that surrounded the creative aspects of the Cotton Club shows. She remained at the club until 1934, staging shows and "mothering" the young chorus girls. Hyacinth Curtis, one of the Cotton Club Girls, credits Webb with teaching the girls how to look good while they were dancing. She taught hand movements and dramatic expressions to those who were not highly talented dancers. In the process, she discovered several budding talents, including the singer Lena Horne and Estrelita Morse, who would become famous

as an exotic dancer. Webb is credited with the dramatic staging of the number "Stormy Weather," which catapulted a singer from Chicago named Ethel Waters to fame at the Cotton Club. She also choreographed acts for other exclusive Harlem clubs—for the Plantation Club beginning in 1925 and for Connie's Inn beginning in 1933.

Elida Webb's career as a choreographer came to an abrupt end in the middle 1930s. Some believe it was because she had cancer, although she underwent a successful operation and lived until the age of seventy-nine. Others suggest that she retired after she was raped and had to suffer the publicity of the trial of her attackers. She was so embarrassed that she withdrew from public life and lived quietly with her family for several years. Eventually, she started a dancing school on Broadway for small children and for stars who wanted to learn new dance routines. One of her most devoted pupils was the white actor George Raft, to whom she taught the steps for his well-known dance number "Sweet Georgia Brown."

In 1947, she got married for the second time. Garfield Dawson, who danced under the name George Dawson and called himself "The Strutter," had worked as a waiter at the Cotton Club when Webb was the choreographer there. Webb had known him for years, and it is likely that she helped him stage his acts. At one point during their marriage, Webb was asked to stage a show in Saratoga Springs, New York, for five hundred dollars. Dawson was offered a job as a men's room attendant at the hotel. But when Dawson learned that there was also an opening for a ladies' room attendant, he persuaded his wife to

Whites-only clubs such as the Cotton Club flourished in Harlem during the 1920s when liquor was illegal and downtown whites saw Harlem as a playground. All the entertainers were light-complected blacks, and dancing was a big part of the lavish floor shows. *Author's Collection.*

take that job instead because she could make more money at it. As a ladies' room attendant, she could make two thousand dollars for the summer, which gives some indication of the comparative living standards for choreographers and domestic workers in those days.

In later years, Webb worked for Ethel Waters as dresser and secretary and reportedly was poorly treated by Waters, who was not well liked in the business. However, Webb never complained. Much later, as Waters' career was failing and she was suffering from severe depression, she called Webb and asked to move in with her. But Margaret Webb, Elida's sister, threatened to move out if Elida said yes.

Webb died in New York in 1975. Her husband survived her.

Had there been greater opportunities for black choreographers during her era, Elida Webb might have made a more important mark on the history of American dance. Her choreography of the Charleston in *Runnin' Wild* was the only major contribution she made to the art. Her work at the Cotton Club and other exclusive Harlem clubs was steady, but it did not allow for a great deal of creativity. The dances she choreographed for the Cotton Club Girls broke no new ground. Clarence Robinson, the black choreographer who replaced her at the club, was the one who brought in tap dancing. As Bessie Dudley, who did specialty numbers at the club, once explained, for the Cotton Club Girls there was no "hard" (technically difficult) dancing because they were supposed to impress patrons with the way they looked rather than with fancy movements. It was the specialty dancers who did the "hard" dancing.

Clarence "Buddy" Bradley

There were so few opportunities for black choreographers in the United States in the 1920s and 1930s that Buddy Bradley had to go to Europe to get the recognition he deserved. But before he left the United States, he coached and created dance routines for a great number of white stars, including Fred Astaire, Lucille Ball, Mae West, and Eleanor Powell.

Clarence "Buddy" Bradley was born in Harrisburg, Pennsylvania, in the early teens of this century. He was dancing by the age of eight, concentrating on the Charleston and other African-derived dances. His father died when he was very young, and when he was fourteen, his mother also died. After her death, Bradley moved to Utica, New York, to live with a brother-in-law. He got a job as a busboy at a local hotel. But he didn't stay in Utica long. Within three months he was in New York City, determined to make a living by dancing.

He found that he had to work as an elevator operator to pay his expenses, but when he was not working, he could be found hanging out with dancers. He went often to the Hoofers Club, where tap dancers tried to outdo each other and also learn the latest steps. Bradley learned quickly and soon landed a job as a chorus boy at Connie's Inn. Chorus work bored him, but it was a living, and he studied the work of the dancing stars who were featured in the shows at the club.

In 1928, he met Billy Pierce, a white man who wanted to start a dance studio for white stars. The two agreed

to work together, and soon the studio was thriving, for Buddy had a knack for teaching dance, even to people with "two left feet." He became director of the Pierce Studios with a staff of five instructors.

In choreographing dance routines for his white clients, Bradley used combinations of steps, ranging from tap to the Shuffle and Drag and other steps from black dancing. He got most of his inspiration from jazz records. He would listen to the solos and then turn them into patterns of dance steps. He was so successful that he had more white students than he could teach. But he was never asked to choreograph a white show in the U.S., although once he was called in to help out a show that was in trouble because the original choreography was so poor.

Buddy Bradley knew very well that it was racism that kept him out of the big choreography jobs. Thus when Charles B. Cochrane, a British producer, hired him to choreograph a show in London, he did not have to be asked twice. Bradley arrived in London in 1933 and returned to the United States only to visit after that. He choreographed many shows in England as well as in France, Italy, Switzerland, and Spain. Once, in 1939, he had the opportunity to choreograph a Hollywood film. But there were problems with the writing of the film, and he had to return to England before the picture was made. Had the schedule worked out better, he would have been the first black choreographer to do the dances for an all-white American movie. And he might have opened up opportunities for other black choreographers in the United States. But for Bradley the opportunities were in Europe, and that is where he remained.

There were other important black choreographers during the 1920s, 1930s, and 1940s, including Charlie White, Frank Montgomery, Sammy Dyer, and Willie Covan. But they all had to be content with choreographing black shows. They coached white dancers, but only privately.

As was the case for black choreographers, there were no black dance "stars" in the United States for many years. The best black dancers were well known among blacks, and among white dancers, but not to the general public. The dances themselves were the stars. The first black dancer in the twentieth century to become a star in his own right was Bill Robinson, and real stardom came to him only after he'd been dancing for more than forty years.

Bill "Bojangles" Robinson

Robinson was born in Richmond, Virginia. Records of black births were not regularly kept in the South in those days—primarily because few black babies were born in hospitals, most of which were white and would not admit blacks. And like many entertainers at that time, Robinson tended to understate his age, but most evidence points to an 1878 birth date.

Robinson left Richmond when he was about twelve years old, but not before he had accomplished four things that would become hallmarks of his career. First, he had acquired the nickname "Bojangles" from childhood friends. It was a corruption of Boujasson, the name of a hatmaker whose tall beaver hat "disappeared" one day, and appar-

ently wound up in Robinson's possession. Second, he had coined the term "copacetic," which meant that everything was even better than fine and dandy. Later, the term was included in Funk & Wagnalls' dictionary. Third, beginning at about age six or eight, he had developed the dancing talent that would eventually make him famous. And fourth, he had developed the "stair dance" that later became his trademark.

His first steady job was as a "pick" (short for pickaninny) in an 1892 minstrel show called *The South Before the War*. Later, he worked in vaudeville with a variety of partners, dancing and doing comedy routines. At the time, there was no black vaudeville circuit; the first one, the Theater Owners Booking Agency, would not be organized until the middle teens. White theaters had an unwritten rule called the "two-colored rule." White show managers did not believe that blacks had enough brains to entertain whites as solo acts. There were exceptions, like Juba, but usually the only time a black performer came close to performing solo was in tent shows, carnivals, or medicine shows. So for Bill Robinson, it was necessary to have a partner in order to work.

The longest-running partnership he enjoyed was with George Cooper, although at first he got little opportunity to dance and had to play the clown. Over time, Robinson got more opportunities to dance and started to receive equal billing with Cooper. The partnership broke up in 1914, after more than twelve years, primarily because of Robinson's gambling habit and his penchant for squandering both his money *and* Cooper's.

After that, Robinson took the bold step of going solo, and aided by a clever manager named Marty Forkins (the two would be in business together until Robinson's death), he became the first black solo entertainer in vaudeville. He introduced the stair dance into his act in 1918, but since few theaters had steps leading from the orchestra area to the stage, he was unable to do that stair dance regularly until he had his own portable staircase built, probably about six years later.

Others had done stair dances before him. An act called the Whitney Brothers had done a musical stair dance in 1899, and the team of Mack and Williams did a single, double, and triple stair dance in 1915. What distinguished Bill Robinson's stair dance was his showmanship. His stair dance, when perfected, involved a different rhythm for each step—each one reverberating with a different pitch—and the fact that he had a special set of portable steps enhanced his claim to originating the dance. By the spring of 1921, it was a standard part of his act. He even tried to secure a patent on his stair routine, although the U.S. Patent Office in Washington, D.C., declined his application.

Robinson traveled the vaudeville circuits all over the country, rarely having a day off. But he didn't mind. He used to say that his feet did their best work when they were tired. He loved to dance, loved to entertain. But traveling as much as he did was very hard for a black man. There were signs outside hotels and boarding houses that read, "No Negroes, Jews, or dogs allowed." He could not enter most white restaurants. Trains were segregated.

And he was never a headliner, which was also due to racism, even though he had far more talent than many white individual acts and teams who were billed above him. In fact, the only place in the newspaper where he made headlines was on the sports page, for Robinson had a particular talent for running backward, and would often compete against forward-running athletes in special contests. According to the *Guinness Book of World Records*, he held the record for running the mile backward until Paul Wilson broke it in New Zealand in 1977.

Not until 1928 did Bill Robinson get the chance to appear on Broadway. He starred with Adelaide Hall and others in Lew Leslie's *Blackbirds of 1928*, an all-black musical that Leslie hoped would be as popular as *Shuffle Along* had been seven years earlier. Robinson did not appear until the second act, but when he did, he seemed to electrify the stage. The routine he did was similar to his vaudeville act: He sang and danced to a number titled "Doin' the New Low Down." He tapped up and down a flight of five steps. He flashed his sunny smile. He very cleverly made the audience pay attention to his feet by watching them himself. For the first time, white downtown audiences really began to appreciate the finer points of tap, and they were enthralled. Suddenly, he was established as a Broadway headliner.

Experts in tap say that Bill Robinson was not the greatest tap dancer in the world, nor was he the most original. But he had a way of investing the steps he did with his own particular style. In their book *Jazz Dance*, Marshall and Jean Stearns described that style this way: "Sand-

wiched between a Buck or Time Step, Robinson might use a little skating step to stop-time; or a Scoot step, a crossover tap which looked like a jig; hands on hips, tapping as he went, while one foot kicked up and over the other; or a double tap, one hand on hip, one arm extended, with eyes blinking, head shaking, and derby cocked; . . . or a broken-legged or old man's dance, one leg short and wobbling with the beat; or an exit step. . . ." All the while he told jokes and stories and did imitations—a mosquito's hum, a trombone—his comedic timing as perfect as his tapping. And on top of all that, he was physically very appealing. About five foot seven, he was in the habit of compensating for his slight build by hunching up his shoulders, which made him look vulnerable. His face was open and good-natured, his smile infectious. Charles "Honi" Coles, another tap dancer, once said, "In a sense, Bo's face was about forty percent of his appeal."

From then on, his legend kept growing. His name became familiar to almost every American household. He appeared in more Broadway shows, but after about 1930, the era of the "colored revue" had ended, in large part because there had been too many poorly staged shows. The Depression was another reason. After the stock market crashed in 1929, the nation slid into such a serious economic depression that two thirds of Manhattan's theaters were shut down. The popularity of tap dancing was also on the wane. But that did not affect Robinson's popularity, which was independent of changes in taste.

Robinson went to Hollywood, where he became Shirley Temple's most famous co-star. He appeared with the white

Bill "Bojangles" Robinson was the most popular tap dancer in American history. He didn't invent the stair dance, but he made it famous. *Author's Collection.*

child star and danced with her in several movies. Seven-year-old Shirley Temple and fifty-six-year-old Bill Robinson grew very close. Although she was very young, even she realized there was something odd about the fact that when they went to Palm Springs, she and her family got to stay in the main hotel while Bill had to stay in the chauffeur's quarters—with his *own* chauffeur.

Robinson rarely complained publicly about discrimination. As a rule, he went along with it, realizing that there was little he could do to change things. But one time in 1934, he became publicly enraged. The New York Society of Teachers of Dancing had invited him to appear at their convention at the posh Waldorf-Astoria Hotel, but no one remembered to alert the employees of the hotel that he was coming. When Robinson arrived with his dancing shoes, the elevator operator would not let him on. In a rare public display of anger, Robinson socked the man in the face, saying, "I'm Bill Robinson and I came here to teach your white teachers to dance."

In 1936, his fiftieth year in show business, Robinson headlined at the first show the Cotton Club staged after its move downtown from Harlem to Broadway and 48th Street. At one point in the late 1930s, he was starring in the Broadway musical *The Hot Mikado* and headlining at the Cotton Club, performing in five shows a day. He later appeared in *Stormy Weather*, the first all-black Hollywood movie produced by a major studio, and starred in touring revues. He began to suffer from cataracts and had a series of mild heart attacks in the last couple of years before he died. Even so, he continued to perform at benefits until

just a few months before his death in 1949. He was seventy-one.

No other entertainer performed in as many benefits as Bill Robinson. Nor was any as generous with his money. Because of his generosity and his gambling, he was broke when he died; but his friends in and out of show business saw to it that he had a lavish funeral. He was the most beloved entertainer of his time—unofficially called "Mayor of Harlem," and the recipient of countless awards. In the years following his death, his image became tarnished by charges that he could have done more to improve conditions for black people, that he had been an "Uncle Tom" because he had not used his position to push for better treatment. But no one was prouder of being black, nor more dignified, than Bill Robinson, and with his dignity and talent he did a great deal to increase respect for his race.

Robinson was married three times. His first marriage was brief. His second, to Fannie Clay, lasted twenty-one years. In 1943, he divorced Clay and married a much younger woman, Elaine Plains, to whom he was still married when he died. He never had any children.

Ordinary black people had an especially difficult time during the Depression. They were "last hired and first fired," and not long after the stock market crash, Harlem was no longer the happy playground that whites had enjoyed for a decade. Harlem had also become dangerous, not because of the people who lived there but because of mob infighting. Prohibition was repealed in 1933, and organized crime lost its major source of income—illegal

liquor. In response, mobsters started fighting each other over control of prostitution and illegal gambling and the other rackets that were left. After a couple of shoot-outs in Harlem, white downtowners stopped going uptown to play.

The Harlem Renaissance essentially ended, too, with the stock market crash and the repeal of Prohibition. But some black entertainers continued to enjoy considerable popularity and got steady work in the big downtown clubs. As mentioned earlier, the Cotton Club moved downtown in 1936, and remained open, putting on ever more lavish black revues, until 1940. Connie's Inn, another big Harlem club during the Renaissance, also moved downtown, and new clubs like the Latin Quarter opened up in the midtown area. Bands like Duke Ellington's and Cab Calloway's continued to be popular, as did a variety of dance acts.

The majority of dance acts in those days were two-person dancing teams—Buck and Bubbles, Anise and Aland, Swan and Lee, Rufus and Richard, Son and Sonny, Renee and Estella. There were a number of brother dancing acts, including the Bohee Brothers and the Berry Brothers and the Four Step Brothers. One of the most famous pairs was the Nicholas Brothers.

The Nicholas Brothers

Fayard and Harold Nicholas were born in 1918 and 1924, respectively. Fayard was born in New York City, but moved with his parents to Philadelphia when he was three. His parents were musicians—his father played the drums

and his mother played piano—and had gotten a job managing the pit band at the Strand Theater in Philadelphia. They called the band the "Nicholas Collegiates." Three-year-old Fayard was deposited in the front row while his parents worked. He watched some of the greatest black vaudeville dancers rehearse and perform, and he began picking up some tap dance steps. Harold was born three years later, and it was often Fayard's job to look after him. As soon as Harold could walk, Fayard started teaching him to dance.

At first, Harold couldn't seem to dance with both feet. He could get the timing right with one, but not with the other. Then one day, while he was drying the dishes, he finally managed to do a Time Step on both feet, and from then on, his older brother had no trouble teaching him. Soon, they were doing acrobatics as well as tap dancing. Harold often said that Fayard was his only tap dancing influence, and that not even Bill Robinson had made as much of an impression on him as his older brother, whom he idolized.

Their parents realized that the two boys were talented and cute, and encouraged them to develop a dance act. "We started as professionals right away," Fayard once said, "and no amateur shows or anything like that because they knew the business and they knew so many people in the business." They made their debut in 1931, when Harold was just seven, dancing on *The Horn and Hardart Children's Hour*, a popular radio show in Philadelphia. The great advantage of tap dancing was that it produced *sounds* and so could be featured on the radio. From there, it was a short tap to theaters where their combinations of spins,

flips, twists, and tap dancing brought them considerable local fame.

The following year, the Nicholas family moved back to New York, primarily so that the boys could get more exposure in show business. Fayard was fourteen and Harold eight when they made their debut at the Harlem Cotton Club. They were exceptionally popular with the society crowd that patronized the club, as well as with the older stars (Harold's tenth birthday was celebrated backstage at the club). But their popularity didn't derive simply from their youth and attractive appearance. Their small size was probably part of their appeal and continued to be, since Fayard never grew taller than five feet four inches and Harold no taller than five feet two. But according to Fayard, the real reason for their popularity was their talent, and their poise. "From the beginning we danced like men. Most children will be out there huffing and puffing, they'll fall down and get up again and people say, 'Oh, isn't that cute?' But with us, we were out there doing it like men." They played at the Cotton Club on and off, both uptown and downtown, for the next eight years, and during most of those years they traveled to and from the club in a limousine with their mother, who usually wore a mink coat.

They made their first Broadway appearance in *Ziegfeld Follies of 1936*. George Balanchine, who later became one of the most famous American choreographers of the twentieth century, was the choreographer for the revue, and he took the Nicholas Brothers with him to the next show he did, Rodgers and Hart's *Babes in Arms*.

During the 1940s, they appeared in a succession of Holly-

wood films. They starred with Betty Grable and Carmen Miranda in *Down Argentine Way*, in which they ran up a wall for two steps, then backflipped into a spectacular split. They leap-frogged over one another down a staircase in *Stormy Weather*, which starred Lena Horne. They appeared with Glenn Miller's Orchestra in *Orchestra Wives*. The choreographer for *Orchestra Wives* was Nick Castle, and he loved working with the Nicholas Brothers, according to Harold, because they would do whatever he thought up. "We didn't care about breaking our legs or anything. We were young, eager. We just did it." It was Castle who helped them create their most stupendous move: Fayard ran up a wall and landed in a split while Harold ran up another wall and did a backflip before he, too, came down in a split.

They regretted never having a chance to act in those films, but in those days the only acting roles open to blacks were as servants or jungle natives. The "specialty numbers" that black entertainers did could easily be cut out by southern censors before the movies were shown in theaters in the South. But they took some pride in their popularity in the movies. Fayard once said, "People sat and *waited* for our parts. The whites had the roles; we had the popularity."

During their Hollywood period, both Fayard and Harold got married. Fayard married Geraldine Payton, who was living in Chicago at the time, after knowing her only a month. Harold married Dorothy Dandridge, one of the Dandridge Sisters, a group of three singers that included two sisters and one non-sister. Both couples bought homes

in Los Angeles and each had one child—Fayard and his wife had a son, Harold and his wife a daughter. Both couples eventually divorced.

Their film career was interrupted in 1944 when Fayard was drafted into the army, where he served thirteen months. In his absence, Harold did a solo specialty act in nightclubs, but he once said that he always imagined Fayard dancing right next to him.

After Fayard was discharged from the army, the brothers did get a chance to act in an all-black musical. In *St. Louis Woman*, they played horse-racing jockeys, which was appropriate casting, since they were both very small and since most jockeys in the early days of horse racing were black.

The brothers influenced many white dancers. They worked with Gene Kelly in *St. Louis Woman*, during which Kelly learned several of their routines. He would use these routines later in his own act. Donald O'Connor did a wall-climbing step in *Singing in the Rain*, but he did not come off the wall in a split.

By the end of the 1940s, tap dancing had started losing its appeal in the United States, so the Nicholas Brothers and their wives went to Europe. In 1948, they gave a Royal Command Performance for the King of England and traveled throughout Europe. They split up in 1951, when Harold decided to stay in Paris and Fayard returned to the United States. He toured the United States and Mexico as a single act. Reunited in 1964, they played Las Vegas and made a number of TV appearances.

In the 1970s, when black movies were popular in Holly-

wood, both brothers got a chance to act. Fayard co-starred in the 1970 film *The Liberation of L. B. Jones*, and five years later Harold co-starred in *Uptown Saturday Night*.

By the 1980s, a renewed interest in tap dancing led to a renewed interest in the Nicholas Brothers. They were featured at the 1981 Academy Awards ceremony. They served as dance consultants to shows and movies where tap dancing was featured, including the 1984 movie *The Cotton Club*. They starred in a Las Vegas revue that was billed as a tribute to the old Cotton Club. In the mid-1980s, Harold starred for nine months in *Sophisticated Ladies*, another Las Vegas revue, this one based on a hit Broadway show. In 1988, he made a few special appearances as a singer.

Fayard, whose problems with severe arthritis forced him to have both hips replaced, no longer dances. In 1989, he was one of the choreographers of the Broadway show *Black and Blue*. Harold, the younger brother, continues to work as often as he can, and he appeared in the 1989 film *Tap*, starring Gregory Hines. He enjoys teaching young people and is concerned that young blacks don't seem very interested in tap. "That's unfortunate, because it really belongs to us," he says. "They [black dancers] just have a thing about it. An Uncle Tom thing, because it belongs to the old days. But an art form is an art form."

Tap dancing is indeed an art form, but somehow it is usually seen as an art form only when it is performed by white dancers. In the 1980s, a TV special called *That's Dancing* was produced. Its star was Gene Kelly. Gene Kelly is a very talented dancer, but the show neglected to empha-

66

The Nicholas Brothers, Harold, left, and Fayard, dance in a scene from *St. Louis Woman. AP/Wide World Photos.*

size the important role of black tap dancers in film and theater. Signs that this emphasis was changing occurred in 1989, when the Broadway musical revue *Black and Blue*, and the Hollywood film *Tap*, signaled new interest in black tap dancing.

Still, blacks had a much easier time gaining acceptance as tap and jazz dancers than they did as "concert dancers." It wasn't until the 1930s that individual blacks began to carve a niche in that field.

Chapter 4

Black Concert Dance Is Born, But the Toes Keep Tappin': The 1930s

Until the 1930s, American dance was not seen on the concert stage. Dancing was regarded as part of musical-comedy routines, or in connection with singing, or as part of a variety show. But an entire program devoted exclusively to dance was a major innovation. In the 1930s, black and white dancers began giving such programs, the first "modern dance" performances. In modern dance, neither whites nor blacks were first, so white and black concert dance were developing at the same time.

The New Negro Art Theatre Dance Group

The first professional black dance company was founded in New York in 1931 by Helmsley Winfield, who was born

in Yonkers, New York, in 1906 or 1907. His mother was a playwright, and he began his career as an actor. After appearing with a company of dancers in his mother's play *Wade in the Water* at the Cherry Lane Theatre in Greenwich Village in 1927, he became interested in dance. He danced in an Oscar Wilde play titled *Salome* and then decided to form his own company.

The group was composed of eighteen dancers, including Edna Guy, who had studied with the white dancer Ruth St. Denis; Ollie Burgoyne; Randolph Sawyer; and Frances Dimitry. Its first performance was at a benefit show in Yonkers, and at the time the group was called Bronze Ballet Plastique. By the time of its debut concert in 1931, however, the name had been changed to the Negro Art Theatre. The debut concert was billed as the "First Negro Dance Recital in America" and took place at the Theatre-in-the-Clouds on top of the Chanin Building in Manhattan on April 29, 1931. The production was supported or aided by several well-known white dancers, including Ruth St. Denis, Felicia Sorel, Gluck Sandor, and Grace Hooper. The program included solos by Edna Guy that had nothing to do with African dance—"Figure from Angkor-Vat" (a temple in Cambodia) and "Temple Offering." But there was a suite that was based on African themes and on Winfield's compositions "Negro," "Ritual," and "Jungle Wedding" (which he danced with Frances Dimitry). There was also a suite based on the Negro spirituals "Weeping Mary" and "Git on Board, Little Chillun." One critic wrote that these suites "constantly brought to mind the rhythm that is the Negro's heritage" and that the recital was "the

outstanding novelty of the dance season." The critic called the concert a novelty because he did not regard dances with African or black themes as serious dancing. Still, the concert was reviewed, and the company, which was also sometimes called the New Negro Art Dancers, received its first publicity.

The group performed other concerts whenever they could. When they had trouble getting engagements, Winfield would lift the spirits of the dancers by telling them, "We're building a foundation that will make people take black dance seriously." In 1933, Winfield and his company joined the Hall Johnson Choir in a production of Johnson's play *Run Lil Chillun*. That same year, Winfield obtained the greatest opportunity of his career—to direct the ballet in the Metropolitan Opera Company's production of Eugene O'Neill's *Emperor Jones*.

It was an event that caused considerable controversy, for no individual black dancer, much less an entire company, had ever danced at the Metropolitan. But the O'Neill play on which Louis Gruenberg's opera was based was about a black man, and while the title role was performed by a white singer in blackface (Lawrence Tibbett), the Metropolitan believed it was only fitting to have some blacks in the cast for this production. Winfield brought his own company to the production, and not only directed it but also played the role of the Witch Doctor in the production, thus becoming the first black to dance in a featured role at the Metropolitan. His performance was critically acclaimed, and he might well have gone on to even greater heights. But sadly, while he was dancing at the Metropoli-

tan, Winfield came down with pneumonia and died at the age of twenty-six or twenty-seven.

An annual Helmsley Winfield award is given as part of the Celebration of Men in Dance at the Thelma Hill Performing Arts Center in Brooklyn, New York.

The company disbanded after Winfield's death, but some of its members went on to make their own marks in the world of dance. Edna Guy became famous for her Negro "Dance Spirituals," and Eugene Sawyer integrated the Dance Center that white dancers Gluck Sandor and Felicia Sorel had formed. Over the years, Sawyer also danced in a variety of Broadway musicals, and he and Edna Guy performed together on different occasions, appearing in 1943 in the number "Boxing Ballet" in the production *Carmen Jones*.

Hampton Institute Creative Dance Group

Hampton Institute is a black college that was founded in 1868 by an ex-Union officer named Samuel Chapman Armstrong. Its purpose was to educate the children of former slaves. By the 1920s, most of its students were middle class, but because there were so few career opportunities open to blacks, Hampton, like other black schools, emphasized practical training courses, especially teacher training, over liberal arts courses. By the middle 1920s students at Hampton and other black colleges were com-

plaining that the schools should upgrade their curricula so that graduates could compete on an equal footing with white college graduates. The unrest led to student strikes on many black campuses, including Hampton.

This unrest on the part of the students may have spurred Charles H. Williams, Director of Physical Education at Hampton, to seek administration approval to form a creative dance group at the Institute. Williams was interested in movement, and especially in dance. He had read widely on the subject of dance, and believed that African and African-American dances were marvelous examples of pure bodily expression of emotion. He felt that the students would benefit greatly from a dance program, not only because it would help them with their physical coordination but also because it would give them a new pride in their heritage. With the help of Charlotte Moton Kennedy, an instructor of physical education at the Institute who was also interested in dance, he founded the Creative Dance Group for Hampton students.

Many of the students were physical education majors, and so they were naturally well coordinated. But they were still amateurs. What made the programs of the Hampton Creative Dance Group so innovative was the choice of material presented. The programs covered the range of African-American dance, from the Juba and the Cakewalk to the Buck and Wing and popular dances of the day. But they also included African dances based on demonstrations by African students attending the Institute.

Some of the most memorable were "Mamah Parah," which was danced on stilts, and "The Fangai Man," which

was about magical customs. In "Wymomamie," which dealt with African marriage customs, a Liberian student named Frank Roberts danced the role of the groom.

Charles Williams also choreographed dances that told stories from black American history, like "Middle Passage," which dealt with the slave trade and included dance renditions of black spirituals and folklore.

The Hampton Institute Creative Dance Group made its first appearance outside the Hampton campus in Richmond, Virginia, in 1935, and from then on it was in considerable demand locally. Meanwhile, Williams began to spend portions of his summers developing his skills in choreography at Bennington College, a white girls' school in Vermont, which sponsored an annual Bennington Festival of Dance. The Hampton group, which by 1937 was composed of forty young men and women, made its New York debut in November of that year at the Young Men's Hebrew Association, in a program sponsored by the YMHA Dance Theatre. The following week it began its first northern tour at Bryn Mawr College. From time to time, the Creative Dance Group appeared with native African dancers. One of the most popular was Toniea Massaquoi, a young Liberian dancer who also appeared at Radio City Music Hall in New York.

Not only did the group bring to the public a wider appreciation of African and African-American dance as an art form—not merely an entertainment form—it also helped the image of Hampton Institute. An official press release from Hampton stated, "At work or at play, and after work, the African and his descendants in America have been

74

alike afflicted with what the Negro poet, Paul Lawrence Dunbar, called 'itchin' heels,' heels ready to caper in almost any kind of dance at a moment's notice. Seeing that this is an original and native endowment, Hampton desires to provide opportunity for its development." While this statement would make Hampton public relations people cringe today (it smacks of "Uncle Tomism"), there is no question that the Institute was proud of its dance group and eager to exploit its popularity for the benefit of the college. The Hampton group spawned similar groups at other black colleges, including Spellman in Atlanta, Fisk in Nashville, and Howard in Washington, D.C.

Asadata Dafora

In the early 1930s, a dancer leaped onto the American scene who would change forever public perceptions of African dance and of black concert dance. Asadata Dafora was born Austin Asadata Dafora Horton on August 4, 1890, in Freetown, Sierra Leone, in Africa. He studied music and dance in Germany before coming to the United States in 1929 at the age of thirty-nine. He used the last name "Horton" from time to time because his great-grandfather had been a slave in Nova Scotia and had taken his master's last name, and probably also because it was a name that was more familiar to Americans than his African name.

On arrival in New York, he worked first as a musician, but within five years he had produced and created what

he called an opera, titled *Kykunkor*. Subtitled *The Witch Woman*, it told the story of a hapless bridegroom on whom a curse is placed, and of his attempts to remove it. The opera was lavish and colorful, and the music, singing, and dancing were so exciting that, as with *Shuffle Along* more than a decade earlier, the audience could hardly keep still. In addition to Dafora, there were several other African male dancers in the cast, including Abdul Assen, as well as black American women dancers, among them Frances Dimitry and Alma Sutton. All danced with great exuberance the various authentic dances of joy, jest, challenge, war, and festival.

For white Americans, the greatest impact of *Kykunkor* was that it portrayed an African as a regular human being. It had rarely occurred to most whites that an African could be anything but a savage and brutal creature. For black Americans, the greatest impact was in seeing authentic African dances performed on the concert stage. Dr. Alain Locke, the black philosopher, critic, and chronicler of the Harlem Renaissance, wrote that "it represents the beginning of an entirely new and healthy adaptation of the pure African tradition of ritual, dance, costume, and music after several generations of mere sentimental dabbling in African local color and cheap pseudo-African effects."

Dafora participated in several Federal Theater Project productions (the FTP will be discussed in more detail in the next section), including the Harlem FTP's famous Haitian *Macbeth* in 1937 and a revival of *The Emperor Jones* in 1939. In 1938, four years after *Kykunkor*, Dafora presented a second dance-drama titled *Zunguru*. While it was a better production than the first, it did not have the same impact.

Asadata Dafora continued to perform in dance programs, but he never was able to mount another lavish, full-scale stage production. He did, however, continue to create memorable dances with African themes in a series of Carnegie Hall concerts, and for many years he worked with a company that included at various times actresses Josephine Premice and Esther Rolle as well as dancers Abdul Assen, Zebedee Collins, and Randolph Sawyer.

Over the years, he produced seven more full-length pieces, including *The Shingandi* (1945), *A Tale of Old Africa* (1946), *Festival in New Africa* (1954), and *The Valley Without Echo* (1957). His last two major choreographed works, both performed in 1959, were *Afra Ghan Jazz* and *Program for African Dance Festival*. Both were connected with the surge of nationalist feeling in Africa, as well as the emerging independence of many African nations from the European powers that had ruled them as colonies.

In 1960, Dafora returned to a newly independent Sierra Leone to serve in that country's ministry of culture, but he was seventy years old and in failing health. He was forced to return to New York for treatment, where he died in 1965, at the age of seventy-five.

Perhaps no one more than Asadata Dafora inspired so many black American dancers to view dance as an expression of life, as a means of interpreting emotion and ideas, and as a way to celebrate the African heritage. In the 1970s, there was a renewal of interest in his works. Esther Rolle and Zebedee Collins organized revivals of his group works and solos for the company of Charles Moore, thus exposing his art to a whole new generation of young American dancers.

The Federal Theater Project

The Federal Theater Project also helped in the development of black dancing with African themes. The FTP was a part of the Works Progress Administration, an agency established under the administration of President Franklin Delano Roosevelt. The WPA began in 1935, at the height of the Great Depression, and was an attempt to do something about the massive unemployment of the time. WPA programs gave jobs to all kinds of workers, from ditch diggers, house painters, stonemasons, and forestry workers to artists, photographers, writers, and actors. Some people wondered why artists should be given jobs, but the Roosevelt Administration understood that artists could starve just as easily as ditch diggers. And the point of the WPA arts programs was to pay artists to create art for all people, not just the rich and educated.

One of the programs created was the Federal Writers Project, for which writers produced guides to different parts of the country. They also collected oral histories of various regions and participated in a huge program of interviewing elderly black people who remembered slavery. Under the Federal Arts Project, artists painted murals for post offices across the country. And the Federal Theater Project, which was organized in 1935, offered plays and musicals for ordinary people to see.

Although the WPA programs in the arts were not a major force in music and dance as they were in the fields of theater, art, and writing, the Federal Theater Project did help in the development of black dance.

Unlike other WPA arts programs, the Federal Theater Project established separate theatrical groups, called "units," for blacks and whites. The reason was that while there were many black actors and actresses, there were few black playwrights, directors, set designers, producers, and stage managers. Having separate units would allow blacks to get experience in these areas. This was not segregation against blacks, but for the benefit of blacks. As for the segregation that prevailed in theaters in many parts of the country, the officials of the FTP would have no part in that. Hallie Flanagan, the white woman who directed the FTP, was very progressive. In one of the early organizational meetings of the FTP, it was decided that there would be no segregated seating in any theater that was part of the FTP, nor would any FTP traveling company have segregated traveling accommodations.

In New York, the Harlem unit of the FTP was called the Negro Theater Project and was housed in the Lafayette Theater. The Negro Theater Project staged a unique, all-black production of *Macbeth*, the play by William Shakespeare. The play as Shakespeare wrote it was set in Scotland, but this version was set in Haiti. The original play had featured witches. In this version, there were witch doctors and voodoo. A young white director named Orson Welles was hired to direct the production, for at the time no black directors had enough experience to do so. He discovered a touring African dance group stranded in New York, who were unable to afford their passage back to Africa, and he signed them up. He also employed the talents of Asadata Dafora. The musical

score for the show was filled with voodoo drums and witches' cries, and the jungle sets were exotic and eerie. *Macbeth*, which opened in April 1936, was a critical and popular success, and after a seven-month run in New York went on national tour.

The African dancers in *Macbeth* were crucial to the excitement and exoticism of the production, and by 1937, an African unit of the Federal Theater Project had been established. Asadata Dafora's 1934 dance-drama *Kykunkor* is said to have been an inspiration for this unit, although the Federal Theater Project was not organized until the following year. In 1937, the African unit produced a dance-drama called *Bassa Moona*, directed by Momodu Johnson.

The Federal Theater Project gave a young dancer and anthropologist named Katherine Dunham her first job as a choreographer. As dance director for the "Negro unit" of the Chicago branch of the FTP, she staged dance numbers for productions of *Emperor Jones* (in which Asadata Dafora participated) and *Run Lil Chillun*. The Chicago unit also staged one of her own dances, "L'Ag'Ya," which was based on the folk dances of the Caribbean island of Martinique, where she had recently done anthropological fieldwork. Katherine Dunham will be treated more fully in the next chapter.

The Federal Theater Project lasted a mere four years. From the beginning, it had enemies in Congress, which was responsible for funding the various WPA projects. Its policies of integrating its activities and even its social affairs did not appeal to racist Congressmen, one of whom charged that "racial equality forms a vital part of communistic teachings and practices." There was great fear in those

days that the doctrine of communism on which the Soviet Union was based would infiltrate the United States, and there was some justification for this fear. During the Depression, the Communist Party did gain in popularity among unemployed workers and intellectuals. It was true that the FTP included some communists and other people sympathetic to communism, in both white and black units. But the FTP was hardly infested with radicals. It was doomed by its own forward-looking principles of racial equality. Funding for the FTP was withdrawn by Congress in 1939. Two years later, the WPA as a whole came to an end, as the Depression ended and the United States entered into World War II.

While the FTP lasted only four years and had no dramatic impact on the development of black dance, it nevertheless gave jobs to black dancers and helped to inspire interest in dances with black themes, both African and Caribbean. By the late 1930s, this type of dance was fairly well established as an art form. However, there was one area where black dancers were not at all established, even in the 1930s, and that was in ballet.

One of the reasons why Helmsley Winfield's dancing in *Emperor Jones* at the Metropolitan Opera in 1933 caused so much controversy was that whites found it difficult to accept the idea that blacks could excel at classical "European" dances like ballet. John Martin, the powerful drama critic for *The New York Times*, wrote in 1933 that "Negroes cannot be expected to do dances designed for another race." Such reactions and comments were variations on the same theme: "Better stick to your own dances. You

81

are natural-born dancers, your dances require no training, and training will cause you to lose originality and spontaneity. Besides, how dare you try to copy a white's art?" It was an admonition heard many times before by blacks, and not just black dancers. Black writers were not supposed to be able to write about white subjects. Black singers were only supposed to be able to sing the blues and jazz, not opera. Black musicians were not supposed to have the ability to play classical music, which was said to be much more difficult than jazz.

That there were not a lot of black dancers interested in ballet until the 1920s and 1930s is understandable. There was no native ballet tradition in America, and it wasn't until the 1930s that a white ballet company was established. Furthermore, ballet was a more formalized type of dance and required lessons, and many black families could not afford them. Even so, by the middle 1920s, there were some eight children's dancing schools in Harlem, among them schools run by Otis C. Butler and Mary Bruce. And by the 1930s, black dancers had begun to break out of the creative straitjacket in which whites wanted them to remain. The early black pioneers in ballet believed that all kinds of music and feeling could be expressed in dance, and that pure expression had no color.

First American Negro Ballet

The first black concert dance company was started by a white man, a German named Eugene von Grona, who had been a student of the dancers Mary Wigman and

Roxy Rothafel. He was trained in modern dance and in the course of his training learned about black dances. He wondered why blacks had not entered the field of serious concert dance and believed that with the proper training, blacks could excel as professional concert dancers. In 1934, he ran an advertisement in a Harlem newspaper in which he offered free dance training to talented dancers. One hundred and fifty people responded to the ad, bringing with them great enthusiasm, if little experience. Over the next three years, von Grona selected a company numbering twenty-two.

He groomed that company by teaching them the principles of dance that he had himself learned in Germany. And although von Grona called the company the First American Negro *Ballet*, he deliberately allowed his students to move in ways that were natural to them and tried not to impose his style or too many classic ballet techniques upon them. For example, he did not have them dance *en pointe* (on their toes).

As he prepared them for their debut performance as a professional dance troupe, von Grona allowed his students to select much of the music to which they would dance, and the result was a varied program that ranged from the classic *Firebird* by Stravinsky to compositions by Duke Ellington and W. C. Handy, two great jazz and blues composers and musicians.

At last, on November 21, 1937, just a couple of weeks after the New York debut of the Hampton Institute Creative Dance Group, the First American Negro Ballet debuted at the Lafayette Theater in Harlem. They received mixed reviews. Some critics referred to the production as a "stu-

dent recital," knowing full well that the company had been practicing for three years. They called the dancing "inept," the attempts at classical ballet steps by black dancers "incongruous." But others wrote that some compositions, notably "Southern Episode," which was based on the music of Duke Ellington and W. C. Handy, were handled with "genuine finesse and consistent ensemble unity."

Since no film exists of the First American Negro Ballet, it is difficult to tell which critics were right. White critics of the time approached the program with their own biases against the ability of blacks to do "white dancing." As one critic wrote, "Von Grona was swamped with congratulations. Through most of them ran the note of amazement at the way members of the troupe had temporarily abandoned the Suzy-Q and other forms of terpsichorean hotcha [popular dance] to go on to conquer a manner of dance expression once strange to them."

After their debut, the group appeared in concerts with symphony orchestras and at the Ballet Congress, as well as in their own concerts. In 1939, two years after their premier performance, the First American Negro Ballet appeared as a "Swing Ballet" in Lew Leslie's *Blackbirds of 1939*, which starred Lena Horne and which closed after one night. Not long afterward, von Grona disbanded the company, for he could not get bookings or find sponsorship. Still, short-lived as it was, the company was a trailblazer in the field of black ballet.

Whites, even those who understood and appreciated dance in all its forms, were still very uncomfortable with

Southern blacks who migrated to northern cities in the 1920s and 1930s brought their dances with them. The Jitterbug was one that caught on with the larger population. *Author's Collection*.

the idea of blacks doing anything but black dancing and felt most comfortable seeing black dancers doing the popular, jazz dances of the day.

There were still plenty of those in the 1930s. The Lindy Hop continued its popularity from the 1920s. It was named after Charles Lindbergh, who made the first trans-Atlantic airplane flight in his *Spirit of St. Louis* in 1927. The dance had little to do with airplanes. However, women who danced it managed to take flight quite frequently, with the help of their male partners. It was a potpourri of a dance, containing steps from all sorts of other dances, most of them originating among black Americans. For example, it included a step called the Geetchie Walk, which John Bunting, in an article titled "Dances of Harlem," described as "strutting proudly along and slightly wriggling from head to feet, the head shaking rather like a musical timer."

The Suzy-Q, mentioned earlier, enjoyed brief popularity in the 1930s after being introduced at the downtown Cotton Club. It was a tap dance with a smooth slide step. By the late 1930s, the newest dance rage was the Jitterbug, created for the rhythms of the new swing jazz, which was in 4/4 syncopated time. Like the Lindy Hop, it was a combination of different dance steps and was heavy on acrobatics.

The Nicholas Brothers were at the peak of their popularity in the later 1930s, as were a variety of other dancing duos. Still popular, too, were individual novelty dancers, among them Peg-Leg Bates, who would have been hard-pressed to find a partner who could match him.

Peg-Leg Bates

He was born Clayton Bates in Fountain Inn, South Carolina, in 1908. When he was four, his mother and his father, a cotton farmer, were divorced, and he and his mother moved to Greenville, South Carolina, where his mother got a job as a nurse for a white family. Even as a youngster, Clayton did odd jobs to help with family finances or to make the money to buy something he wanted. In 1918, when he was ten, he heard that there was going to be a county fair in Greenville, and he was determined to have a new suit of clothes to wear to the fair. The United States had entered World War I the previous year, and most of the men were off to war. The ten-year-old had no trouble getting a job at the local cottonseed mill. His job was to get on top of a pile of cottonseed and cave it in, so it would drop into the conveyor.

"I didn't know the job," he later recalled, "so I caved in this pile of seed and slid down with it. It slid me right into the conveyor and I hit the auger, which crushes the seed into meal. In that way I lost my left leg and two fingers off my right hand."

It was hard for the young boy to adjust to the loss of the leg. He had been a great first baseman in baseball until the accident; now he was made umpire. He was aware that the other kids felt sorry for him, and he didn't enjoy being pitied. So he was determined to show them that he was just as good as they were, if not better. He asked his uncle to make him a peg leg. "I put that leg on, and I used to walk and run five miles a day, jumping

across ditches, way out in the woods by myself." After a while, he got so he could run and jump as well as the other boys. Everyone, even his mother, started calling him Peg-Leg, or Peg, and that was okay with him.

One evening, his uncle was in the kitchen and in a good mood, and he started dancing. Peg-Leg got up and imitated the older man and found that he could make a beat with his good leg and match it with his peg. Soon, he was dancing in amateur shows at the Liberty Theater, the local black theater, and winning all the prizes. He ran away with a black traveling show, which soon broke up. All together, he ran away with six such shows, all of which disbanded soon afterward.

After being stranded for the sixth time, Peg-Leg got together with two friends, one who could sing and one who could play the guitar, and the three started going from town to town performing on street corners. In 1926, he left his two friends and joined Eddie Leonard's *Dashing Dinah* company, which traveled all across the country. When the company reached New York in 1928, Leonard got Peg-Leg a week at the Lafayette Theater in Harlem, and he stole the show. He was held over for a second week and could have stayed longer if he hadn't been given the chance to appear on Broadway.

His style, which was fully developed by this time, was primarily tap dancing, but it was a kind of tap dancing that few could duplicate. "I depend on novelty steps a two-legged man couldn't do," he once explained. "In one routine I leap five and a half feet in the air and make a complete turn. If I'm in good trim I can leap

as tall as I am, five feet eleven."

Lew Leslie wanted him for *Blackbirds of 1928*, in which Bill "Bojangles" Robinson got his first Broadway break. Peg-Leg was a great hit in *Blackbirds* and later accompanied it to Paris, where the show played twenty-two weeks at the Moulin Rouge club.

Returning to New York, he played the big clubs, like the Paradise and Connie's Inn, and traveled the vaudeville circuits—or what was left of them, since vaudeville was going out of fashion by the late 1930s. In 1934, he went to London with another version of Lew Leslie's *Blackbirds*, and he made a second trip to London in 1936. By this time he had thirteen different peg legs, "one to fit every suit, all colors," and was wealthy, but he still kept the original peg leg his uncle had made for him.

In March 1938, Peg-Leg Bates headlined at the downtown Cotton Club for the first time, stomping around the stage and singing "I'm Peg-Leg Bates, that one-legged dancing fool." His big number in the 1938 Cotton Club show was "Slappin' Seventh Avenue with the Sole of My Shoe." He headlined at the opening of the Club Zanzibar in New York in 1944 and starred in another Broadway show, *Bronze Follies*, in 1946.

Peg-Leg Bates continued in vaudeville and toured with the Count Basie Orchestra and the Ink Spots, a singing group, until the end of the 1950s. After his retirement from the stage, he opened a resort for blacks in the town of Kerhonkson in upstate New York, and happily entertained in the shows at his own nightclub. Bates is alive at this writing.

By 1940, American tastes in entertainment had undergone a change. Lavish, Ziegfeld-type shows were no longer as popular, even on Broadway, and it followed that they could not last long in nightclubs. The Cotton Club closed its doors in June 1940, a victim of the changing tastes. Tap dancing was no longer as popular. Ballet was now the rage on the concert stage. The 1936 show *On Your Toes*, choreographed by George Balanchine, started the excitement, and by the time *Oklahoma!* premiered in 1943, ballet had taken over. But it was white ballet, not black ballet. It would take many more years before black ballet would be accepted.

But black modern dance and ethnic dance continued to surge in popularity during the war years, as we will see in the next chapter.

Chapter 5
Black Pioneers in Modern Dance: The 1940s

Black modern dance became well established during the 1940s. Modern dance is different from ballet in several respects, the most important being that it does not look to European models for its movement techniques, but rather to the expressive needs of the individual. The ballet is a formal, classical style of dance, which recognizes five basic positions and which requires that any movement begin and end with one of the five positions. Modern dance is expressionistic, and so any position necessary to create the desired effect is acceptable. The ballet emphasizes leaps into the air, while modern dance uses the ground as a source of stability and strength. Female ballet dancers almost always wear toe shoes, while modern dancers perform in their bare feet to better feel the energy from the floor. In ballet, the torso is strongly controlled,

with the spine arched, while in modern dance the torso moves in a more supple manner.

The white pioneers of modern dance worked in the early part of the twentieth century into the 1930s, fighting considerable prejudice on the part of the dance establishment and the American public. People like Ted Shawn, Ruth St. Denis, and Isadora Duncan were the real trailblazers, followed by Martha Graham and Lester Horton and others who established various schools of modern dance. They followed a very democratic line in their companies, with no one comparable to the prima ballerina of a ballet company, and once it became acceptable to the public for black dancers and white dancers to appear onstage together, they integrated their companies with ease. Lester Horton's was the first integrated modern dance company, but many others followed.

At first, however, blacks had to form their own modern dance companies, and in some ways this was good both for them and for modern dance. Left to their own devices, they discovered movements that they might not have been able to express in the company of white dancers. Modern dance as a whole benefited from the pioneering efforts of the early black modern dancers.

The earliest known black modern dance group was formed in Minneapolis, Minnesota, in 1940. A dancer named Bernice Brown performed modern dances with an integrated group she had developed at the Modern Dance Center. Two of her best-known pieces were *Negro Lament* and *Statement for Peace*; however, the group did not become well known outside the Midwest.

Two years later, in 1942, Wilson Williams formed a sixteen-member company called the Negro Dance Company. Its premier performance in January 1943 featured two works that he had choreographed—*Prodigal Son* and *Spring Ritual*—as well as works by two prominent white dancers of the time, Felicia Sorel and Gluck Sandor. Sorel was also a co-director of the Negro Dance Company. Unfortunately, the Negro Dance Company did not last long, but it was another attempt to create a company that could be a fount of creative black talent.

Williams had been a teacher and lecturer on dance at the Harlem branch of the YMCA, and he believed strongly that black dancers needed an established school or company where they could be trained and from which they could go out and found their own companies. Not many years after Williams' attempt failed, Katherine Dunham succeeded.

Katherine Dunham

Katherine Dunham is without question a giant of black concert dance. She put black dance "on the map," and it has been there ever since. She was born in 1909 in a suburb of Chicago, and raised in Joliet, Illinois. Dunham was an entertainer from an early age, putting on performances of singing and dancing at home and at church. She once said, "I think I was born interested in dance. As far back as I can remember, I was interested in motion." She was also interested in anthropology before she knew

what the word meant—as a youngster, she was fascinated with Native Americans and formed a secret club at school called the Eagle Eye Society, based on a symbol she had seen in a book about Native Americans.

In high school, she was a member of the Terpsichorean Club (in Greek mythology, Terpsichore was the Greek goddess of the dance). She was also president of the Girls' Athletic League and played center on the girls' basketball team. At the University of Chicago, she had no idea what she would major in, so she took basic liberal arts courses. On the side, she took ballet lessons, and in early 1930, when she was barely twenty-one, she opened her own dance school with the backing of two white dancers whom she had met.

She called the company of dancers she formed from her students the Ballet Negre (Negro Ballet), and from the beginning she was determined to show through her company her belief that black people had a special dance style. But the effects of the stock market crash in New York in 1929 soon reached Chicago. She began to lose students, and then her two backers had to withdraw their support because they had to go back to their own careers. She was forced to close her school. Meanwhile, she had married a fellow dancer named Jordis McCoo.

One day she attended a lecture given by a professor in the Department of Anthropology at the University of Chicago. The subject was the bits and pieces of African culture that had survived in the New World after slavery, and these included dances. Dunham was excited to learn that popular dances in the United States, like the Lindy

94

Hop and the Cakewalk and the Black Bottom, could be traced back to Africa.

Her reaction was not typical of most black people in those days, who were ashamed of their African heritage because most popular films and books portrayed Africans as savages. One had to go to a library and find some musty old book that hadn't been taken out in years to find the truth: that there had been great societies in Africa, with rich and powerful kings, with civilizations more advanced than those in Europe at the time, and with proud cultural traditions. Dunham found these books, and read about Africa, and became even more excited. She wanted to share her excitement with young people, so she opened two more schools. Both were failures. Black parents did not want their daughters to learn "primitive dances"; they wanted them to learn ballet, so they would be graceful and "refined."

Meanwhile, Dunham had taken all the anthropology courses she could, but she was disappointed in their lack of attention to dances of different cultures. She realized that the anthropologists who had studied these cultures had not been dancers and couldn't appreciate the dances as a dancer could. So she applied to the Rosenwald Fund in Chicago for a grant to study the dances of various cultures herself, and received the grant.

In the summer of 1935, at the age of twenty-six, Katherine Dunham began an extended study trip to the West Indies. In Jamaica, she studied the culture of the Maroons (descendants of slaves who had escaped from their Spanish masters in 1655). On the island of Martinique, she was

Katherine Dunham ran dancing schools in Chicago in the 1930s. She wanted to teach African dance, but the parents of her students wanted them to learn ballet. *Author's Collection.*

able to witness the war dance called Ag'Ya and other dances that had been done on the island as far back as anyone could remember. In Trinidad, she saw part of a Shango ceremony (Shango was the god of lightning worshipped by the Yoruba people in West Africa and brought to the New World by Yoruba slaves). In Haiti, she was initiated into a *vodun* (voodoo) cult and got so caught up in one particular dance that she momentarily forgot who and where she was. She fell in love with Haiti.

After a year, she returned to the United States and the University of Chicago, having accomplished what she had set out to do. She had gathered material on the customs and ceremonies of people of African heritage. She had learned dances that seemed to her to link the dances of American blacks with those of Africans. On the personal level, she had discovered her own proud heritage and gained an understanding of her African roots.

Dunham was awarded a bachelor's degree in anthropology and felt that she ought to go on for further degrees. But what she really wanted to do was dance, and that is the path she chose. She believed she knew what real ethnic dancing was, and wanted to spread the word, or in this case, the movement. As she once explained:

You must know the entire complex, the musical instruments, the rhythms, the songs and what they're used for and how they're used, the language, and the interrelationships among all the elements in this immense cycle that goes with a single dance. So-called ethnic dancers today, who just passed through some

place and picked up a couple of things, are not real ethnic dancers. From my own anthropological training, I've learned that you practically have to put yourself into the skin of a person if you're going to claim to know anything about him or her. If I learned anything from my trip, it was that I couldn't come into a culture as a lady anthropologist who knew dance and leave with any real knowledge of that culture's dances. It just wouldn't be the real thing. In fact I'm still after the real thing.

She made her New York debut at the Young Men's Hebrew Association in 1937 in a *Negro Dance Evening*. Then she got a job as dance director of the Negro Federal Theater Project in Chicago. The opening recital was called *Ballet Fedre* (Federal Ballet) and included a piece she choreographed, a ballet based on the dance she had seen in Martinique, called "L'Ag'Ya."

Dunham's version of the traditional fighting dance was a dance-drama, with a story line. A young man is jilted for another man by the woman he loves, and he tries to break up the happy couple by using a magic charm obtained from the king of the zombies (the "living dead" of Caribbean voodoo). The woman falls under the spell of the love charm and goes into a dancing frenzy. The two men dance a duel.

The action of the ballet was melodramatic, and the climax was especially powerful. The recital was so well received that Dunham took the bold step of hiring a professional manager to book her and a troupe of dancers in cities across the United States.

John Pratt, who had done scenery and costumes for the Federal Theater Project, joined Dunham's troupe in

Katherine Dunham applied her studies in anthropology to the dances she choreographed and made "ethnic dance" acceptable to the larger public. *Author's Collection*.

the same capacity. He was five years younger than she, and white, but they were in love and they refused to let their lives be run by public opinion. Dunham obtained a divorce from Jordis McCoo and married John Pratt in 1940.

A job choreographing a show for the New York Labor Stage in 1939 gave Katherine and John the opportunity to establish themselves in New York. On February 18, 1940, she and her troupe made their off-Broadway debut in a show of their own creation called *Tropics and Le Jazz Hot* at the Windsor Theater. It included elements from a variety of cultures: a Cuban rumba, a Mexican rumba, and two Peruvian pieces, as well as one called "Island Songs." It also included a suite called *Le Jazz Hot* and a folk ballet called *Br'er Rabbit and de Tah Baby* that featured black American dancing. The next morning's newspapers were filled with rave reviews. Critics called her "the first pioneer of the Negro dance" and the first to present black dance as a serious art.

What made Dunham's company and her own dancing so memorable, however, was their excitement. She combined her anthropological knowledge with great imagination and show-business flair. She took authentic dances from Africa, Latin America, and the United States and choreographed them like theater. She entertained at the same time as she instructed. She once said, "I believe there is a certain cosmic rhythm of which we are all a part," and the dances she choreographed were bigger than life, so full of energy that they threatened to explode from the confines of the stage.

Dunham herself was an exceptionally skilled dancer who appeared to draw her rhythms from the center of a volcano.

100

She danced with wild abandon and emphasized the sensual aspects of primitive dancing, sometimes to the embarrassment of staid audiences. The critic John Martin once wrote about a Dunham number, "Its movement is markedly uninhibited and certainly it is nothing to take Grandma to see, but it is an excellent piece of work." Especially shocking to some American audiences were the frankly sexual hip-swinging movements in Dunham's choreography. But she would point out, "African movement is pelvic movement . . . just as movement in the neck, arms and torso is East Indian. It is natural and unselfconscious to the blacks. . . ."

Overnight, the Dunham Dance Company was in demand all across the country. Within a few months they had made their debut on Broadway in the all-black musical drama *Cabin in the Sky*, staged by the famous choreographer George Balanchine. After that show closed on Broadway, it embarked on a national tour. And after that, Dunham and her troupe went to Hollywood, where they appeared in several movie musicals. A year in Hollywood was enough for Dunham, and for the next two years she and her troupe toured widely in all parts of the country except the South, where a black troupe would not have been accepted. But, as other black artists before them had learned, it was hard being on the road all the time, for even in the North transportation and lodging were often segregated. Moreover, Dunham was now in her middle thirties and past her prime as a dancer. So she returned to New York and started another school.

The Katherine Dunham School of Dance, which opened its doors in 1944, was a place where students were taught

Katherine Dunham choreographed the dance sequences and performed with her troupe in *Stormy Weather*, the first all-black film produced by a major Hollywood studio. Bill "Bojangles" Robinson also starred in the film. *Author's Collection*.

not just dance steps but also philosophy, sociology, and anthropology. Young people would learn the customs and languages of other peoples so they could really live the dances of other cultures. The school grew quickly. About one quarter of the student body was white, nearly half were children, and quite a few were from foreign countries.

While running the school, Dunham also kept her dance troupe going, partly in order to pay the expenses of the school. They toured in Mexico and in Europe and Latin America, to great acclaim. Dunham continued to dance with the troupe, despite severe arthritis. She had operations on both knees to remove cartilage that had built up from years of dancing. Her physical condition affected her dancing, but she managed to turn her disabilities into an advantage. She learned to make the most of the subtle movement, the single expressive gesture.

She was anything but subtle in the way she managed her troupe, however. Her personality was as explosive as her choreography, and her financial and health problems did not make her any easier to get along with. But she had such energy, such an ability to inspire, and such a strong sense of herself that many dancers stayed with her in spite of the disadvantages of doing so. This strength came from an inner light, which not only illuminated but warmed everything and everyone around her. Under her tutelage, students learned not just to dance the movements of other cultures but to feel those movements in their souls.

Unfortunately, Dunham was unable to keep her school open because of financial difficulties, and she was forced

to close its doors in 1954. But in more than a decade, the school had provided training for a whole generation of young dancers and had spread the gospel of the Dunham Technique across the nation and around the world.

She continued to provide valuable training and experience to the young members of her troupes, which she formed and disbanded over the years as her finances and physical and mental health demanded. And she continued to be a major influence in dance, creating Broadway revues every few years, including *Bambouche*, which premiered in 1962. The following year, she opened another school, but it was a short-lived venture. After receiving an invitation to choreograph and stage the opera *Faust* at the University of Illinois, Carbondale, she and John closed the school and moved to Illinois.

While at Carbondale, Dunham became interested in East St. Louis, a poor ghetto that had been the focus of riots, racial resentments, delinquency, and poverty. With her characteristic energy, she was determined to establish the Performing Arts Training Center in East St. Louis in the hope of replacing crime and delinquency with discipline of body and mind and determination to work for a goal. After several years, she managed to secure funding for the center, which continues today to offer hope to the young people of East St. Louis and which has spawned a number of gifted and successful professional dancers.

In the late 1980s, much of Katherine Dunham's choreography was revived, most notably by the Alvin Ailey American Dance Theater. Funded by foundation grants, the Ailey company re-created her major works, complete with scenery and costumes. Dunham served as a consultant,

104

helping to make her works live again. While most of the original productions were never recorded on film, these Ailey company versions were carefully filmed to create a record for future generations.

Dance critics of the 1980s were intrigued by the works. Wrote Jack Anderson in *The New York Times*, "[Ms. Dunham] knew she had to entertain—and entertain she did. But some of her works now seem almost compulsively energetic. Indeed, a few are more interesting for their gusto than for their formal complexity. Nevertheless, the Ailey company demonstrated that these dances can still set audiences cheering."

Many of the most famous black dancers of the past forty years owe their success to Katherine Dunham.

Talley Beatty

Talley Beatty was a member of the first Katherine Dunham troupe, the nine dancers who traveled from Chicago to New York to perform in the *Negro Dance Evening* at the Young Men's Hebrew Association in 1937. He was with her again when the Dunham troupe performed *Tropics and Le Jazz Hot* in New York, although one critic didn't think much of what he called Beatty's "serious dallying balletic technique."

After that, he performed in a variety of media, from a dance film called *A Study in Choreography for Camera* in 1945 to a revival of *Show-boat* in 1946, in which he starred with a young dancer named Pearl Primus, to a minstrel ballet called *Blackface* the same year. *Blackface* was presented

by the Ballet Society, which later became the New York City Ballet.

He rejoined the Dunham Dance Company for its tour in Europe in 1948 and was one of several dancers who left the company in Paris. Another was Eartha Kitt, who went on to become a successful nightclub singer in both Europe and the United States. Beatty formed his own dance company and toured Europe and the United States in a show called *Tropicana*, which was clearly based on the kinds of revues that the Dunham troupes presented.

With his own company, Beatty was able to do more choreography, in which he excelled. *Tropicana* included a suite of dances called *Southern Landscape*, whose themes were black life in the Deep South. Beatty soloed in the second dance of the suite, called "Mourner's Bench," and the same critic who in 1940 had criticized his technique had nothing but praise for him now, calling the solo brilliant and a tour de force and characterizing Beatty's style as having simplicity and integrity.

Beatty disbanded his dance company after about five years, but he continued to choreograph some memorable works. Thanks to a grant from the Lena Robbins Foundation in 1959, he created a balletic work titled *The Road of the Phoebe Snow*, which dealt with the famous train that was part of the Lackawanna Railroad. To music by Duke Ellington and Billy Strayhorn, the thirty-minute work was a suite of related dances that told the story of life on the wrong side of the tracks. Critic Clive Barnes called it "one of the great achievements of jazz dance."

Jazz dance was Beatty's forte. The following year, he premiered *Come and Get the Beauty of It Hot*, a suite of

106

dances to music by Dizzy Gillespie, Charlie Mingus, and Gil Evans, all noted jazz musicians and composers. His next major work was the movement for Jean Genet's drama *The Blacks*, which had an extended off-Broadway run. From this he adapted one number, "Look at All Those Lovely Red Roses," for concert use.

During the early 1960s, Beatty choreographed *Danse au Nouveau Cirque* (*Dance at the New Circus*) in Paris and, back in the United States, *The Migration* and *Toccata*. His 1967 work *Montgomery Variations* used injustices against blacks and the civil rights movement as its themes, especially the bus boycott by blacks in Montgomery, Alabama, in 1955. In 1969, his piece *The Black Belt*, which dealt with the horrors of ghetto life, was premiered by the Alvin Ailey Dance Company. By that time, he was artist-in-residence at the Elma Lewis School of Fine Arts in Roxbury, Massachusetts.

In 1968, he had choreographed *The Black Belt* and a revival of *House of Flowers*, a show that had first appeared on Broadway in the early 1950s and that had given a number of young black dancers their starts. His work in this musical comedy led him to more such shows, and in the early 1970s, he choreographed the dances for several, including *But Never Jam Today*, *Billy Noname*, *Croesus and the Witch*, *Ari*, and *Bury the Dead*. Perhaps the best known of his musical comedy works was the Broadway show *Don't Bother Me, I Can't Cope*, directed by Vinnette Carroll, which enjoyed a long run on Broadway.

In the middle 1970s he choreographed *Caravanserai* and *Tres Cantos* (*Three Songs*).

Over the years, Beatty did a variety of work, as most

dancers must in order to make a living. He appeared at international dance festivals, taught dance in several schools, danced with the Ballet Society and with other companies, choreographed whenever and whatever he could, and managed on occasion to produce his own programs. He was best known for his gritty depictions of the hardships of black life, portrayals that had a powerful impact on his audiences and on young developing dancers.

Pearl Primus

Like Katherine Dunham, Pearl Primus was both a dancer and an anthropologist, and like Dunham, she brought a much-needed authenticity to black dance. She was born in Woodstock, Port of Spain, Trinidad, in 1919, where her grandfather, a descendant of the Ashanti people of Africa, held the distinction of head dancer of the country. When she was two years old, she moved to the United States with her family. She grew up in New York City and attended Hunter College High School and Hunter College, where she received her undergraduate degree. She then enrolled in graduate school at New York University as a premed student in psychiatry, but she needed to work to support herself. In addition to being a switchboard operator, she worked in the wardrobe department of the National Youth Administration, which at the time was preparing a group of Lindy Hoppers to appear on a joint program sponsored by the New Dance Group. At the last minute, one of the dancers didn't show up, and

Primus was chosen to fill in. She stole the show with the muscular power of her dancing and the amazing quickness of her feet.

Soon afterward, Primus managed to obtain a working scholarship at the New Dance Group. She cleaned the studio, and received instruction in return, on an hour-by-hour basis. She was not a stranger to the dance, for her family was proud of its dancing tradition, and her mother had taught her many of the native dance forms of Trinidad. But it was at the New Dance Group, where she trained under Charles Weidman and LaBelle Rosette, a specialist in Caribbean dance forms, that she discovered the joy of movement and her own exceptional ability at it.

Struggling to overcome the conflicts over her own identity that were a result of racial discrimination, Primus began to study African history and culture, particularly African dances. At this point in her career, she had not done any fieldwork, and she was not yet an academically trained anthropologist. But she visited museums and read books and consulted African friends in order to understand authentic African dancing as fully as she could. She also decided to major in anthropology and enrolled in Columbia University to work for a Doctorate of Philosophy in Anthropology.

Meanwhile, she began to choreograph dances for herself. Her first composition was titled *African Ceremonial*, which she presented in her first appearance as a professional dancer with four other young dancers. The program was appropriately titled *Five Dancers*, and was performed at the YMHA in February 1943. She also choreographed

109

"Strange Fruit," which referred to the bodies of lynching victims hanging from Southern trees, and *Hard Time Blues*.

Her career took a different turn from there. Two months later, she was offered a job at a nightclub called Cafe Society Downtown, the first New York nightclub in a white neighborhood to welcome customers of all races (its slogan was "The wrong place for the right people"). There, the space in which she had to work was no larger than the reach of her arms, but her dancing was as powerful in that limited space as it was in huge halls.

In 1944, Edwin Denby, dance critic for the *New York Herald Tribune*, described her style this way: "As a dancer, she has a unique power and unction in her hips, knees and instep. The leaps can be thrilling, the quickness of the feet a delight. Waist and torso are strong and often beautifully pliant. She has the gift of motion, which controls the body easily in flow."

Among the solos she choreographed for performance at Cafe Society were *Our Spring Will Come*, *Jim Crow Train*, *Ague*, *Study in Nothing*, and *The Negro Speaks of Rivers*, which was based on a poem by Langston Hughes. Her appearances with the Teddy Wilson Band were tremendously popular, and led to her first national publicity with a story in *Life* magazine that featured photographs of her. John Martin, dance critic for *The New York Times*, called her the best newcomer in dance, noting that in that wartime year of 1943 there were more newcomers than usual.

By the time she danced her second concert at New York's 92nd Street YMHA, Primus had two Afro-Haitian drummers accompanying her, the rhythm and intonation of

Pearl Primus was noted for her strong, athletic style of dancing. *Museum of the City of New York.*

their drumming underscoring the roots of her dances. By her third appearance at the Y, she had her own company, which included Jacqueline Hairston and Joe Nash, and a very balanced program ranging from superb African dances through West Indian folk material to nonethnic dances of both serious and comic character.

Her troupe made its Broadway debut in the fall of 1944 at the Belasco Theater, getting mixed reviews. Edwin Denby of the *New York Herald Tribune* faulted the dances of protest that were included in the program—not for their subject matter but for the way in which they were presented. Not long after that ten-day run, Primus felt the need for more fresh material and took time off to travel to the American South, where she lived among the country people and picked cotton. On her return from the South, she starred in a revival of Oscar Hammerstein's *Show Boat*, then went briefly to Mexico City. Still appearing in *Show Boat*, she took leaves of absence to perform with Lawrence Tibbett in the Chicago Opera production of *The Emperor Jones* and to dance at the annual Fisk University Festival in Nashville, Tennessee.

It was at Fisk that Dr. Edwin Embree, president of the recently disbanded Julius Rosenwald Foundation, first saw her. The Julius Rosenwald Foundation had funded Katherine Dunham's field study in the West Indies a decade earlier, and Dr. Embree was interested to know when Primus had last been to Africa. When he found out that she had never been there, he decided that she must go. The Foundation had recently closed its books after twenty-five years of operation, but Dr. Embree made some calls,

and in 1948, Pearl Primus was awarded a grant to do nine months of study and dance recording in Africa, the last and largest grant the Rosenwald Foundation was to make. She began her work in the rain forests and grasslands of Liberia, moved on across central Nigeria, and finished up in Sudan. Wherever she went, she lived among the local people, sharing their lives and learning their languages. She felt an immediate kinship with the dance rhythms, philosophy, and beauty of Africa, and in turn, the Africans accepted her as a long-lost relative. In western Nigeria, she was given the name "Omowale," which meant "child has returned home."

On her return to the United States in late 1949, Primus spent several months doing lecture-demonstrations rather than concerts. She was particularly concerned with bringing her message to black colleges, for black audiences had been taught to be ashamed of their heritage. She was also invited by New York University to enroll in its department of sociology and anthropology, where she began work on a doctoral degree. In July, she re-formed her dance troupe and traveled extensively in the next two years, including a tour to England, France, Italy, and Finland. All the while, she was assimilating the experiences she'd had in Africa, assembling the material, and deciding the best way to present the strengths and beauties of African dance to Americans. The works she choreographed reflected her African experiences—*Fanga* (1949), *Yoruba People* (1950), *Egbo Escapade* (1950), *The Initiation* (1950), *Benin Woman's War Dance* (1950), *Fanti Dance of Fishermen* (1950), *Excerpts from an African Journey* (1951).

113

Like Katherine Dunham, Pearl Primus studied African and West Indian dancing and translated them into modern dance choreography. *Museum of the City of New York.*

Pearl Primus broke up her dance troupe at the end of 1951 in order to concentrate on her anthropological studies. However, she continued to choreograph and to give solo concert performances. In 1953, she spent the summer studying dance in the West Indies, and it was during this trip that she met Percival Borde, a Trinidadian dancer. They were married the following year. The next year, 1955, their son, Onwin, was born.

In the later 1950s, Pearl Primus appeared as a guest artist with her husband's dance company. In 1959, she was invited to Liberia to be director of that country's first Performing Arts Center. Her husband became her assistant, and the family began spending much of their time in Liberia. The job included raising funds for the project, and that effort brought them back to the United States frequently. Whenever she was in New York, Primus worked on her studies at NYU, and by 1960 had completed all the work toward her degree in anthropology except her thesis. In 1961, she and Percival Borde staged and choreographed an African Carnival in New York, which included a performance by Jean Leon Destine, a fine Haitian dancer. They also opened the Primus-Borde School of Primal Dance in New York City, emphasizing in the name of their school the natural, earthy movements they wanted to teach.

In the early 1960s, Primus and Borde went again to Africa, this time under a grant from the Rebekah Harkness Foundation. On their return, they began a unique program in the New York City public schools called "Meet Africa," in which they introduced elementary-school children to Africa through its dances. Primus would perform the Li-

berian Dance of Welcome and Borde would present the graceful, balletlike dances of the Watusi people. They also gave similar programs for adults. Some critics, who remembered the astonishingly athletic dancing of Primus fifteen years earlier, mourned the fact that she now paid more attention to culture than to dance. But the culture of Africa, and the communication of it to Americans, was now her overriding interest.

Over the next several years, under the sponsorship of the Rebekah Harkness Foundation, Primus and Borde took their programs to eleven different countries and participated in several other cultural exchange programs. In 1971, she was given the National Culture through the Arts Award.

By this time, Pearl Primus was fifty-two years old and well past her peak as a dancer. She completed her doctoral degree in anthropology and turned to a career as a teacher, instructing students in anthropology and sociology in Newark, New Jersey; Harlem; and her own alma mater, Hunter College. Percival Borde had been the choreographer for the Negro Ensemble Company in New York since 1969. Together, they opened the Pearl Primus Dance Language Institute in their home in New Rochelle, New York. Primus also worked extensively with the handicapped and the elderly.

In 1979, Pearl Primus was one of four pioneers of modern dance to be honored by the Alvin Ailey Dance Company, and the acclaim she received led her to make a comeback. She gathered together some longtime friends and associates, including the Afro-Haitian drummer Alphonse

116

Cimber; lead dancer Mary Waithe, who had been with her twenty-five years; her own son, Onwin, a percussionist; and of course her husband, and started giving concert performances again, including a number of solos. Each performance included a lecture on the symbolic significance of some of the dances. By including this information, she was able to give each dance a context, which enriched the dances for the audiences.

At this writing, Pearl Primus is in her late sixties. She is a Five-College professor in Amherst, Massachusetts (which means that she teaches at five colleges in the area). Each summer, she travels to Barbados for research on the Spiritual Baptists, a group whose religion is related to the Aladura religion in West Africa and combines rich movement with chanting. While she no longer dances or choreographs, she still teaches African culture at every opportunity and does volunteer work with the elderly and handicapped, demonstrating that through dance anyone can communicate.

While the 1940s are most noted for the development of black concert dance, they are also significant because they were the last gasp for tap dancing. A shift in jazz music was the main reason tap went out of style. During the 1940s, a new, more complicated jazz, called Bop, evolved. As Marshall and Jean Stearns commented in their book *Jazz Dance*, ". . . since most tappers thought of themselves as drummers, the dancers were crucially affected. . . . For the first time in the parallel histories of jazz music and [jazz] dance, the drumming often became

117

more complicated than the dancing." Bop lent itself more to small combos than to big bands, and this, too, affected tap dancers. Some of the large dance halls closed, although in some cases the reason was not the increasing popularity of Bop so much as it was a new Federal tax on dance floors. Smaller clubs became more popular, but there was no room in these smaller clubs for dance acts.

The most successful tap dancers now were those who were able to create an act that did not try to compete with Bop but instead presented an effective counterpoint to it. One team, Coles and Atkins, enjoyed considerable success by dancing more *slowly* than anyone had before—or has since.

Coles and Atkins

Charles "Honi" Coles (the nickname was given to him by his mother) was born around 1921 in Philadelphia and grew up when fast dancing was the rage. Though taller and lankier than the average tap dancer, he made his physical characteristics work for him. Fellow tapper Pete Nugent said he did "centipede steps," in which his legs and feet seemed to pull in opposite directions. In the late 1920s, he joined two brothers named Miller to form the Three Millers and traveled with them to New York in 1931. There they performed at the Lafayette Theater in Harlem, on narrow planks five feet above the stage. Unfortunately, Harlem was by then sinking into the Depression, and the group was unable to get further bookings. Coles went back to Philadelphia, and the two Millers continued on their own as a duo.

The following year, 1932, Coles was back in New York determined to make it, and he worked at a variety of jobs for the next eight years, including a stint with the Lucky Seven Trio, which played the Apollo Theater in Harlem. He finally landed a steady gig as a solo dancer with Cab Calloway's big swing band. It was during his time with Calloway, 1940–1943, that Coles met Cholly Atkins, who had a song-and-dance act with his wife. The two became good friends.

Atkins grew up in Buffalo, New York, and wanted to be a dancer from the moment he saw The Chocolate Steppers, a boy-and-girl act that was traveling with Cab Calloway at the time, at a local theater. At the age of ten, he won a Charleston contest. By 1935, he was traveling with a group called The Rhythm Pals, which got as far as Hollywood before it broke up. Atkins stayed, appearing in eleven major films. He also did behind-the-scenes movie work—he and a group of friends did sound tracks of tap sequences for white dancers.

Atkins returned to New York around 1940 and got a job as a Cotton Club Boy with the big nightclub. Not only did he dance in the chorus, he also choreographed some of the numbers the group did. Next, he and his wife formed a song-and-dance team and traveled around.

In 1943, both Coles and Atkins joined the army to fight in World War II. After the war, they decided to form a team and earn enough money to open a dancing studio. They had not yet danced together professionally, but Frank Schiffman, owner of the Apollo Theater, already knew the dancing of Honi Coles, and gave them their first booking at the Apollo. Schiffman had owned the Lafayette Theater

in Harlem when Coles had made his New York debut with the Three Millers.

Their act lasted six or seven minutes, beginning with a fast number, continuing on with a precision "swing dance," and then with their famous Soft Shoe. Atkins explained that they had three things in mind when they put together the Soft Shoe: "It had to be slower than anybody else's; at the same time, it had to be really interesting; and finally, it had to be so lyrical that it could stand by itself, that is, it had to *sound* just as good with or without accompaniment, so we could do it without music." The act ended with a challenge dance in which each performed his own specialty.

Coles and Atkins performed with nearly all the big bands from 1945 to 1949, and in 1948 had a triumphant tour of England. They added comedy to their act during this time. In 1949, they joined the cast of the Broadway show *Gentlemen Prefer Blondes* and remained for the course of the show's two-year run. Both enjoyed the chance to have a steady job and to stay at home in New York.

By the time the show closed in 1951, jobs for tap dancers were more and more scarce. It was a tradition for them to open the Apollo Theater's new season, but they could not live on what they made from their Apollo engagements. They did summer stock, mostly revivals of musical comedies, and appeared occasionally on television variety shows. Eventually, however, the two were forced to break up their act and seek work separately, mostly behind the scenes, coaching and choreographing.

For a brief time, Atkins went to work as a coach for Katherine Dunham's school of dance in New York and

One of the many tap dancing teams that were popular in the 1940s when tap was the rage was Coles and Atkins. Seen here performing at the Apollo Theater in Harlem in the early 1940s, Charles "Cholly" Atkins is on the left, Charles "Honi" Coles on the right. *Frank Driggs Collection.*

Coles opened a dance studio with Pete Nugent. Neither Coles nor Atkins was happy, and the dance studio was unsuccessful. Coles and Atkins re-formed their act in 1955 and worked for a time as the opening act for the singer Tony Martin in Las Vegas, then spent more than a year working with the singer Pearl Bailey. But after that, they broke up again.

Atkins went back to coaching. In the middle 1960s, he got a job with Motown Records in Detroit, choreographing the stage acts of the company's singers. He taught the Supremes, among others, how to move in unison on the stage. Coles became production manager at the Apollo Theater, where his wife, Marion, had been a chorus girl between 1937 and 1941. In 1976, after sixteen years as manager at the Apollo, Coles got a role in the black Broadway show *Bubblin' Brown Sugar* and toured in Holland with the troupe after the show closed on Broadway. Ten years after that, in 1986, he starred with Tommy Tune and Twiggy in the Broadway revival of *My One and Only*, for which he won both Tony and Drama Desk awards. Coles was the only tap dancer in the history of the Broadway theater to be so honored.

He was seventy-two years old at the time, and the recognition was a long time coming. But he welcomed the revival of interest in tap that had begun in the late 1970s, and was always available to appear in the many television programs and live engagements that were suddenly being created for tap dancers.

He was pleased to see tap live again, having been around when it died in the 1940s. "Tap dancing died completely

122

[in 1943] because along came Agnes de Mille, whom I love dearly, with *Oklahoma!*, and that killed tap dancing. Prior to Agnes, every musical film coming out of Hollywood had the big tap number." Agnes de Mille's introduction of ballet to the musical stage spelled the end for tap, as did the popularity of modern dance in live performance. This was as true for white tap dancers as it was for black, but since black dancers always had a more difficult time getting work than white dancers did, it was hardest for the black dancers. Many of them were not lucky enough to live to see tap come back.

Chapter 6

From Rock 'n' Roll to Ballet: The 1950s

By the 1950s, American blacks were finding more doors of opportunity opening to them. Partly, this was a result of World War II, in which many black soldiers and sailors had fought heroically. It was also the result of directives from the administration of President Harry S Truman. During the Korean War, Truman's administration had issued orders barring segregation in the armed forces, and had strongly advised that more opportunities be given to blacks in other areas of American life. For example, the government suggested to Hollywood producers and directors that more black films should be made.

This change could also be felt in the worlds of music and dance, where blacks were finally getting at least a big toe in the mainstream. In music, *Billboard* magazine stopped calling black records "race records" and inaugu-

rated a new category: rhythm and blues. Rhythm and blues greatly influenced white musicians, and by the mid-1950s, the new music called rock 'n' roll was all the rage.

Rock 'n' roll brought back popular dancing after a virtual blackout of about ten years, from 1945 to 1954. Some of the reasons were mentioned earlier—the same reasons tap dancing went out of fashion: the Federal tax on dance floors and the new "Bop" music that was for listening, not for dancing. Then, too, there were several record boycotts in the 1940s—when musicians went on strike for higher wages and no records with instrumental tracks were produced. This may also have affected popular dancing. Whatever the reasons, rock 'n' roll music brought with it rock 'n' roll dancing, and kids danced as if they had never been allowed to dance before.

In 1957, Dick Clark took his show *American Bandstand* from radio to television. Filmed in Philadelphia, it brought fame to a whole group of "regulars" who started out as average kids from the streets of the city. Millions of teenagers around the country tuned in every afternoon to watch the *American Bandstand* kids do a variety of group dances that became popular. Two of the earliest were the Madison and Birdland, but they were quickly followed by the Bop, Jet, Roach, Wobble, Locomotion, Choo-Choo, and many others.

To people over fifty, there was something strangely familiar about these dances, especially the best of them. The Mashed Potato and the Charley-Bop were a lot like the Charleston, the Chicken a lot like the old Lindy Hop, and so on. The young dancers had no idea that their latest

125

dances were not entirely original. Nor did it matter to white kids that the dances could be traced back to black sources. By the 1950s, large numbers of white teenagers were dancing to black records, and white stars like Elvis Presley were openly citing black performers and musicians as major influences on them. Elvis Presley, in fact, almost single-handedly brought what professional dancers called "eccentric legomania" into the mainstream. Bo Diddley and other black performers had been gyrating in sexually suggestive ways for years, but Elvis Presley did it on *The Ed Sullivan Show* and almost got away with it (the cameras showed him only from the waist up).

But while white Americans, at least the younger ones, seemed more willing to accept black performers and black influences in popular music and dance, there were still many barriers to black performers in more rarefied areas of the arts.

In ballet, efforts to form a permanent black company were still unavailing. Between 1948 and 1956, there were three attempts to form such companies. The first was Joseph Rickerd's First Negro Classic Ballet, organized in 1948. Next was Thelma Hill and Edward Flemming's New York Negro Ballet, founded in 1955. Thelma Hill left the company the following year, and her directorial duties were taken over by Theodore Hancock. Both Flemming and Hancock were English dancers, and Flemming had achieved considerable distinction abroad. Like Eugene von Grona two decades earlier, they felt that the time had come for a professional black ballet company. Also like von Grona, they advertised for young black dancers, and they conducted a six-month search for talent in leading

126

ballet schools from coast to coast. They chose eight young women and eight young men and prepared them for an extensive European tour including eight weeks in the English provinces and Scotland, four weeks in London, and a Continental tour that opened in Paris. But the company failed to get enough bookings in the United States to keep going. In 1959, the company integrated, with Anthony Bass as principal dancer and choreographer, and changed its name to Ballet Americana. In this incarnation, it was more successful. In 1956, Aubrey Hitchins founded his Negro Dance Company, but this, too, was short-lived.

By the early 1950s, blacks were soloists at the two major opera houses in New York City—Mary Hinkson at the City Center Opera Company and Janet Collins at the Metropolitan. The revitalization of the ballet company at the Metropolitan was an especially important event in the dance world, for it had been largely window dressing for the singing stars. Then Zachary Solov took over as dance director and redeveloped the company. He immediately introduced distinguished soloists, some working on a seasonal basis and some appearing as guest artists. Solov saw no reason not to have a black ballerina, and Janet Collins was leading ballerina with the Met for three years.

Janet Collins

Janet Collins was born March 2, 1917, in New Orleans, Louisiana, and grew up in Los Angeles, where she received her early training from Lester Horton and Carmelita Ma-

racci. Her first work as a dancer was with the Hall Johnson Chorale's 1940 Los Angeles production of *Run Lil Chillun*. Later she performed in *Mikado in Swing*. She auditioned for the Ballet Russe de Monte Carlo, but while there was no question of her talent, she was reluctantly told that she was unacceptable because she was black. Either special parts would have to be created for her, or she would have to dance in whiteface. After appearing in her first film, the 1946 *Thrill of Brazil* for Columbia Pictures, she danced her first solo recital in 1947. Based on that performance, she received a scholarship to study composition with Doris Humphrey.

She had more success in New York, where she arrived in late 1948 and made her debut in February 1949 at the 92nd Street YMHA, the same stage where so many other young black dancers had gotten their first big chances. In this debut, she performed two pieces that she had choreographed herself: a Mozart rondo and two Negro spirituals. She made a profound impression on the New York dance critic who was most skeptical of the ability of blacks to successfully perform ballet. In his review of her performance at the 92nd Street Y, John Martin of *The New York Times* wrote, "Miss Collins happens to be a Negro, but she is not fairly to be described as a 'Negro dancer.' That she is aware of racial backgrounds is evident in the spirituals, but they are in every sense dances rather than an exploitation of heritage."

Janet Collins had little trouble getting work after that. She appeared often in early television variety shows, including *The Admiral Broadway Review* and *This Is Show*

128

Business, as well as the Paul Draper and Jack Haley shows. In 1951, she landed a part in the Cole Porter musical *Out of This World*, dancing the role of "Night" and receiving rave reviews from the critics, who described her as a golden dancing girl. That same year, she became the first black prima ballerina at the Metropolitan Opera.

Often, the first black in any field is light-skinned with so-called "regular features" (meaning more Caucasian than Negroid), and Janet Collins was no exception. But in her beauty and grace she distinguished herself and blazed a trail that would enable others to follow her. The first role she danced at the Met was that of an Ethiopian captive in *Aïda*. Ironically, she had to wear dark makeup for the role because her own complexion was considered too light. She later danced the role of a Spanish girl in *Carmen*, but during her time as prima ballerina at the Met, 1951–1954, she also danced roles in operas with distinctly white subjects, such as *La Giaconda* and *Samson and Delilah*.

She continued to study dance while at the Metropolitan Opera and to teach at the School of American Ballet in New York. During the off-season of the Met, she choreographed and toured. Later, after leaving the Met, she returned to California and taught at the Inner City Cultural Center in Los Angeles, where she and fellow dancers Donald McKayle and Jaime Rogers developed a repertory company.

In the 1960s, she taught dance at Manhattanville College in New York State and created group works for her students. In the 1970s, when she was in her fifties, she danced in several solo recitals and choreographed a number of

works, including *Cockfight* (1972) and *Birds of Peace and Pride, Song, Fire Weaver,* and *Sunday and Sister Jones,* all in 1973.

After Janet Collins left the Metropolitan company in 1954, dance director Zachary Solov hired as leading dancers Carmen De Lavallade (who happened to be Janet Collins' cousin) and later, De Lavallade's husband, Geoffrey Holder. Holder and De Lavallade were then, and remain today, the most striking couple in American dance.

Geoffrey Holder
and Carmen De Lavallade

Holder was born in Port-of-Spain, Trinidad, Pearl Primus' birthplace, on August 20, 1930. His parents were upper-class, and both Geoffrey and his older brother, Boscoe, attended schools where properly accented English was stressed. Geoffrey developed a severe lisp and a stammer, and to this day feels that the reason was the rigidly conventional atmosphere in the school.

He idolized his older brother and took up whatever activity Boscoe was involved in. When Boscoe started painting, so did Geoffrey, who found it a much better way to express himself than speaking. By the time he was fourteen, he was exhibiting in local children's art shows, and he sold his first painting at age nineteen.

Boscoe also was interested in dance. In fact, he was considered the artistic one in the family because of his

many talents. Geoffrey took up the dance, too, and was soon performing with Boscoe's dance troupe. He also became interested in choreography and staged three revues for the troupe—*Ballet Congo, Bal Creole,* and *Bal Negre.*

Not until Boscoe left Trinidad to go to London did Geoffrey start to do dance and choreography on his own, taking over his brother's company. He not only choreographed the dances, he also designed and stitched the costumes. By this time, he had dropped out of Queens Royal College and was working as a clerk on the docks in Port-of-Spain. But every chance he got, he was designing and buying materials for costumes for his troupe. In 1952, his troupe was invited to represent Trinidad at the Caribbean festival in San Juan, Puerto Rico. "It was the first thing I had ever done without my brother," Holder recalled years later. "It was freaky for me. I cried like a baby when they gave me a cake onstage (it was my birthday). You have only one real opening night in your life and *that* was mine."

Holder moved to New York in the spring of 1953 and by the fall of 1954 was performing on Broadway in a musical called *House of Flowers,* written by Truman Capote (lyrics) and Harold Arlen (music). There he met a beautiful young ballerina named Carmen De Lavallade. He proposed four days later. She wasn't ready to rush into anything, but after the run of the show ended in 1955, they were married.

Like her cousin, Janet Collins, Carmen De Lavallade was born in 1931 in New Orleans, Louisiana, and raised in Los Angeles, California. She studied ballet locally and joined the ballet company of Lester Horton, with which she performed from 1950 to 1954. During that time, she

One of the most attractive and versatile couples in black dance, Carmen De Lavallade and Geoffrey Holder met when they danced together in the 1954 production of *House of Flowers* in New York. *Museum of the City of New York.*

created roles in *Salome* (1950), *Another Touch of Klee* and *Medea* (both 1951), and *Liberian Suite* and *Dedication in Our Time* (both 1952). Her movement was marked by unusual grace and polish and what has been called a "slow, incandescent fire."

De Lavallade also began a long association with another dancer in the company, Alvin Ailey, who would take over as director after Horton's death. After dancing in three Hollywood movies, she moved to New York in the middle 1950s and worked as a free-lance dancer with several companies before landing a role in *House of Flowers*.

After their marriage, De Lavallade and Holder pursued their careers together and separately. De Lavallade succeeded her cousin, Janet Collins, as prima ballerina of the Metropolitan Opera, where she remained for two years, 1955–1956. She retired to have a son, Leo, and Holder then joined the Metropolitan opera. He made his debut in *Aïda* and was praised by critics for his "enormous dignity" and "majestic presence."

Holder, in addition to his dancing, had pursued his painting and had two one-man shows in New York galleries before he was awarded a Guggenheim Fellowship in art for 1956 and 1957. By this time, his lisp and stammer had disappeared, and the only reason Holder could imagine for this was his own happiness. By 1957, he was rehearsing for a role in the all-black revival of the Samuel Beckett play *Waiting for Godot*. His performance in this nonmusical drama was called by critics "a masterpiece of spectacular delivery." In 1957, he was choreographer for the show *Rosalie*.

Both Holder and De Lavallade danced in John Butler's company: De Lavallade as a principal dancer, Holder as a guest artist. Both also danced in their own recitals. An engagement in 1958 at Radio City Music Hall in New York City featured them both, and after that they did several months of nightclub work together at such places as the Coconut Grove in Los Angeles and the American Club in Miami. Of the two, De Lavallade was considered the finer single talent, but the multitalented Holder was hailed as a twentieth-century Renaissance Man—one who could do many things well.

During the 1960s, Holder appeared in Hollywood films and in 1965 developed a one-man show that he took on the college lecture circuit. Called *Instant Theater*, it was a mix of singing, dancing, and improvised costumes. Ten years later, he was still doing college dates whenever he could. "Speaking at colleges is the biggest glory of my life," he said in 1975, "because of what I could not do as a child."

De Lavallade, despite her classical training, was relegated to modern dance after she left the Metropolitan Opera. At that time, modern dance was not considered an art form equal to ballet, and regardless of talent and training, black dancers with potential for the ballet were not encouraged to perform in classical repertory. She danced with Alvin Ailey's troupe in a number of performances during the 1960s, including the 1961 *Roots of the Blues*, and in Donald McKayle's *Reflections in the Park* in 1964, as well as with the John Butler Company. In 1962, she was co-director of the Ailey troupe on its tour abroad, sponsored by the U.S. State Department. In the late 1960s,

she joined the Yale School of Drama as choreographer and performer-in-residence, staging musical numbers in plays, musicals, and operas as well as acting and dancing.

In the 1970s, Holder became one of the few dancers to do commercials and thus one of the best-known personalities in the dance world. He is still known as "the Un-Cola man" for his 7-Up commercials. He continued to paint and to exhibit in art galleries. He also choreographed two all-black Broadway musicals—*The Wiz* in 1975 and *Timbuktu* in 1978. For *The Wiz*, he also directed and designed the costumes and won Tony Awards in both categories. De Lavallade, in addition to her work at the Yale School of Drama, choreographed several productions for the New York Shakespeare Festival, including the critically praised 1972 production *Les Chansons de Bilitis*.

For many years, the couple have maintained two apartments in a high-rise building on New York's Upper West Side because of their different schedules and habits. But they have remained married and warmly supportive of one another in their various artistic pursuits.

In spite of the success of Geoffrey Holder, there was much resistance to the idea of a black man in American ballet in the 1950s. We have already mentioned that there was resistance to blacks—male or female—in ballet for a long time. John Martin, the prominent New York dance critic, went so far as to write the following in *John Martin's Book of Dance*, published in 1963:

It is an anthropological oversimplification, to be sure, to speak of such a thing as the Negro body, especially when one considers

135

in Africa alone the contrast between the Watusi and the Pygmy. Nevertheless, in practice there is a racial constant, so to speak, in the proportions of the limbs and torso and the conformation of the feet, all of which affect body placement: in addition, the deliberately maintained erectness of the European dancer's spine is in marked contrast to the fluidity of the Negro dancer's, and the latter's natural concentration of movement in the pelvic region is similarly at odds with European usage. When the Negro takes on the style of the European, he succeeds only in being affected, just as the European dancer who attempts to dance like the Negro seems only gauche.

By the time Martin's book was published, several black women had danced principal roles at the Metropolitan Opera. Indeed, Martin himself noted that Janet Collins was the exception to his rule. It is difficult to understand why he did not consider Carmen De Lavallade and Geoffrey Holder as two more exceptions. One wonders how the critic Martin could maintain his theory that the black dancer, by virtue of physical characteristics, could not look "right" dancing ballet, with all the available evidence to the contrary.

It is less difficult to understand the resistance to black men in ballet. The stereotype of the black man did not allow for grace and beauty. Public resistance was particularly strong against black men in integrated ballet companies: There was the sticky matter of the performance of *pas de deux* (dances for two) featuring a man and a woman, and many white Americans would not accept a black man dancing with a white woman. To overcome this resistance, a black male ballet dancer had to somehow

make his audience forget his color, and only a handful have been able to do it. Christian Holder, nephew of Geoffrey Holder, danced with the Joffrey Ballet. John Jones danced with both the Joffrey company and the Harkness Ballet. Arthur Mitchell was the first black male ballet dancer to have had a sustained career with a major, predominantly white, ballet company.

Arthur Mitchell

Born in 1935, Mitchell was the eldest of five children in a poor Harlem family. He attended neighborhood public elementary and junior high schools. Then, prompted by a junior-high-school counselor who had seen him dancing at a social function, he did a tap dance audition and gained admission to the public but exclusive High School of the Performing Arts, now a part of Fiorello La Guardia High School. He did an imitation of Fred Astaire, the great white movie dancer, because it was the only routine he knew.

At this specialized high school, which was the inspiration for the movie *Fame* and its television spinoff, students take courses in dance and music as well as in math, science, and geography. Mitchell took tap, modern dance, and ballet, but as time went on, he found ballet to be the greatest challenge and thus the style that he was most interested in. Still, he was being nudged toward modern dance by some of his teachers. One of his teachers, Mary Hinkson, a black former soloist with the Martha Graham company, disagreed and worried that he would forsake

ballet. She appealed to Karel Shook, who was then teaching at the Katherine Dunham School of Dance, to teach Mitchell ballet technique, and with the help of a scholarship he learned it.

On graduation from the High School of the Performing Arts in 1952, Mitchell had so distinguished himself in dance that he was offered two scholarships. One was to Bennington College, a liberal-arts college containing the best modern dance training school in the country, where he would have been the first male student in the dance department of this predominantly women's college. The other was to the School of American Ballet, the educational arm of the New York City Ballet. His adviser at the High School of the Performing Arts warned him that pursuing a career in ballet would not be easy and reminded him that very few black males had made it in the field. According to Mitchell, "I was told right away I'd have to work twice as hard as anyone in my class to prove myself." But Mitchell loved challenges, and he had decided that his heart was in the ballet. He chose the tougher road.

While studying ballet, Mitchell continued to dance in the modern style as well, appearing with Donald McKayle's company and with the New Dance Group. He also danced briefly in *House of Flowers*, the same production in which Geoffrey Holder and Carmen De Lavallade appeared.

During his time at the School of American Ballet, Arthur Mitchell experienced the racism that had kept many other black male dancers out of the field. White parents objected to his even taking class with their daughters, not to mention dancing duets with them in recital. The school refused

Arthur Mitchell was the first black male principal dancer with the American Ballet Theater. *AP/Wide World Photos.*

to give in to the parents' objections. Mitchell graduated from the School of American Ballet and spent the summer after graduation in Europe. After that, in 1955, he was invited to join the New York City Ballet.

Arthur Mitchell had learned ballet technique well. His movements were technically flawless. But that did not make him better than countless other young male ballet dancers with a command of technique. Mitchell had something more—a special vitality that audiences responded to. Perhaps it derived from his strong sense that he belonged on the ballet stage and that he had surmounted many barriers to get there. "Ballet is a noble way of dancing," he has said. "Is nobility a virtue of the white dancer alone, and not of the black?" Mitchell communicated that sense of nobility, and gained the respect of all who worked with him.

Arthur Mitchell joined the New York City Ballet in November 1955 and made his American professional debut that same month in a ballet titled *Western Symphony*. John Martin, in his review of the ballet for *The New York Times*, wrote simply, "A casting novelty and a debut was the appearance of the talented young Negro dancer, Arthur Mitchell, in the role usually danced by Jacques D'Amboise. . . ." In fact, the presence of Arthur Mitchell in the company caused little public stir.

At the time Mitchell joined it, the New York City Ballet was seven years old. Its roots were in earlier companies established by the impresario Lincoln Kirstein and the choreographer George Balanchine. Kirstein had first brought Balanchine from Russia to New York in 1933 to serve as the key figure in a long-term plan to establish

140

the ballet as part of artistic life in America. Before that time, there was no real ballet tradition in the United States. The first company they formed was called the American Ballet, which later became the Ballet Caravan. During World War II, Kirstein was in the army, and the company disbanded; Balanchine joined the Ballet Russe de Monte Carlo. After the war, the company was re-formed as a private subscription organization called the Ballet Society. Then, in 1948, it joined forces with the new New York City Center of Music and Drama and took the title of the New York City Ballet.

George Balanchine was director of the New York City Ballet, and he quickly came to admire the talents of the young Arthur Mitchell. He was soon choreographing dances specifically for Mitchell. One of the most famous was a *pas de deux* in *Agon*, to a commissioned score by Igor Stravinsky. Mitchell first performed this with the white ballerina Allegra Kent, and went on to dance the piece for more than six years with either Kent or Diana Adams, another white ballerina. Prominent New York dance critic Edwin Denby, writing of *Agon* in the Tenth Anniversary booklet on the company, said that the fact that his partner is white "and Mr. Mitchell Negro is neither stressed nor hidden; it adds to the interest."

That was usually true of the roles that Arthur Mitchell danced with the New York City Ballet. While on occasion he was specifically cast as black, as in *The Nutcracker* and *The Figure in the Carpet*, in most cases he was cast without regard to color. His roles in *A Midsummer Night's Dream* as Puck, in *Arcade*, and in *Creation of the World* had nothing to do with his color.

141

But his career with the New York City Ballet was not without controversy. The company received letters complaining about a black man dancing with a white woman. On more than one occasion, when the company showed up to do television shows, the producers of a show tried to prevent Mitchell from performing. But Balanchine was always firm in saying that if Mitchell did not dance, then the New York City Ballet did not dance.

He was acclaimed in Europe and the Middle East when he toured there with the company. He danced at Covent Garden in London, at La Scala in Milan, at the Paris Opéra, and in major cities from Tel Aviv to Athens to Moscow, where the company danced at the Bolshoi Ballet. Mitchell also performed in Europe as a soloist, dancing the roles of Mercutio in *Romeo and Juliet* in Stuttgart, and of the Moor in *Othello* at the Munich Opera House.

By the late 1960s, he was actively involved in setting up ballet companies in other countries, including Italy, Senegal, and Brazil. In Brazil, he was asked to be the company's permanent artistic director, but while he was thinking it over, the idea occurred to him to form his own dance company closer to home.

Arthur Mitchell, more than any black male dancer before or since him, was successful in transcending the color line. But he still came up against barriers. In an article in *The New York Times* in 1965, titled "Without Regard for Color," the critic Allen Hughes wrote of the *pas de deux* in *Agon*:

Mr. Mitchell and Miss Kent can dance this duet on theatre stages around the world, but they cannot dance together on

television in this country, at least not on commercially sponsored shows, which includes virtually all shows of major significance. Why? Television stations in the South would refuse to carry the shows, and advertisers would not like that. . . . Why does he not perform with other Negro dancers? He can, and he has, but this does not allow him to show the television public what he is famous for—his roles in the New York City Ballet. . . . If he appears on television at all, then, it must be outside the repertory he has worked for a decade to master.

Not until 1968 did Mitchell dance that famous role on television. It was on *The Tonight Show*, with ballerina Suzanne Farrell, and it was a momentous and controversial occasion. It was also close to the end of his professional dancing career, for he left the New York City Ballet in 1970.

Sadly, no black male dancer took his place in the company. While there have been black male dancers in the New York City Ballet since, notably Mel A. Tomlinson, who was with the company from 1981 to 1987, they cannot be said to have followed the trail blazed by Arthur Mitchell. But Mitchell has blazed another trail, for after he left NYCB, he went on to found the first successful all-black ballet company, the Dance Theater of Harlem.

The Dance Theater of Harlem

The idea for a black ballet company came to Mitchell on the day Dr. Martin Luther King, Jr., was assassinated, April 4, 1968. Mitchell was at the airport getting ready

143

to fly to Brazil, and by the time he boarded the plane, King was dead. He recalls, "I sat there the whole time, thinking to myself, here I am running around the world doing all these things, why not do them at home? I believe in helping people the best way you can, my way is through my art. But sometimes you need a splash of cold water in your face to make you see the right way to do it." That was his last visit to Brazil. When he returned home, he set in motion plans for the Dance Theater of Harlem.

He recalls, "I realized from the start that there was little point in putting black kids through the rigors of development in classical ballet if, once trained, they had little chance to perform. I knew we had to have a school, but my primary objective was to hold on to the nucleus of a company. Without the school to provide it with dancers, the company could not exist. But without the company, the school would be meaningless. The dancers must have an example put before them and must also be trained for a real purpose."

For help with his plan, Mitchell turned to Karel Shook, a white ballet master and a former teacher of Mitchell's at the Katherine Dunham School of Dance who had most recently directed a Dutch ballet company. Together, they sought funding and a space for the school and company. From the beginning, the vision was of a black ballet company, and Mitchell was criticized for "segregating" black dancers in a "black ballet." Critics complained that the company would require a black repertory to maintain its identity, for to dance a traditionally white ballet like *Swan Lake* or *Giselle* would be inappropriate. Mitchell paid no

attention to these critics, except to be determined to mount a production of *Swan Lake* one day.

Despite its name, the Dance Theater of Harlem began operations in a loft in Greenwich Village in February 1969. DTH then moved uptown to the basement of the Church of the Master on Morningside Avenue in Harlem; the basement was fully renovated with the help of a $315,000 grant from the Ford Foundation. The troupe began almost simultaneously with the school, which was a highly unorthodox way to operate; however, DTH had to match the Ford Foundation grant, and the only way to raise money was to give performances. On January 8, 1971, just two years after the creation of the school, the company made its debut at the Guggenheim Museum, the young dancers making up with their energy whatever they lacked in technique. Clive Barnes, dance critic for *The New York Times*, called the company "a controlled avalanche."

In the summer of 1971, the company made its first European appearance at the Festival of Two Worlds in Spoleto, Italy, followed by a tour of Italy, Belgium, and Holland. On its return that fall, the company moved into its permanent home at 466 West 152nd Street, a renovated garage and warehouse that had been the gift of Alva B. Gimbel.

In these larger quarters, the school was able to expand its course offerings to include instruction not only in dance but also in costume design and production, music, and, surprisingly, typing. Mitchell had a policy of hiring his students, and since all administrative tasks, including bookkeeping and publicity, were handled on an in-house basis, he saw no reason not to train his own clerical staff.

In 1973, the company made a prize-winning television special titled *Rhythmetron*, and the following year presented its first exclusive New York City season for three weeks at the ANTA Theater. By 1976, the school had a student body of 1,300, the company comprised 27 dancers whose average age was twenty, *and* it had its own orchestra formed by Tania Leon, the young black female musical director of DTH since 1970.

The company's repertory combined the classical tradition with ethnic dance styles and included works by Mitchell himself as well as George Balanchine, Geoffrey Holder, and others. Early on, DTH would have liked to stage productions of the most famous classical ballets, such as *Swan Lake*, but the company did not have either the money or the dancers to do spectacular nineteenth-century ballets. They did the best they could with what they had, and each year DTH became more professional and more respected in the dance world. They played several full seasons in England and were invited twice to perform for the Queen Mother. DTH had a reputation for turning out highly disciplined dancers. The dancer Ben Vereen, who had studied at DTH in its early years, was a star on Broadway, and all the black shows on Broadway—revivals of *Porgy and Bess* and *Guys and Dolls*, as well as new musicals such as *The Wiz* and *Don't Bother Me, I Can't Cope*—had former DTH students in their casts. Within the company itself, although there are no stars, there have been some principal dancers of star quality, among them Lydia Abarca, Virginia Johnson, Lowell Smith, Ronald Perry, and Paul Russell.

Like other black dance companies, the Dance Theater of Harlem received the greatest acclaim in European capitals. Mitchell believes that part of the attraction is the name *Harlem*. "Harlem is a magic word. When you say *Harlem*, it fascinates everyone all over the world. Many times they'll say, 'Oh, are you the Globetrotters?' Or, 'Are you a basketball team?' But a lot of people come and say, 'Ah, it's ballet, but you know they're wonderful.' "

However, with each passing year, DTH has gained greater recognition in the United States. With increased funding over the years, it has been able to mount more ambitious productions. *Swan Lake* was included in its repertory beginning in 1981, and *Giselle* was added a couple of years later.

Giselle became an integral part of its repertory, though not without some alterations. The story, which was originally set in Germany in medieval times, is about a young village woman named Giselle who rejects the sincere affections of an unsophisticated village man in favor of a somewhat mysterious, romantic man with whom she falls wildly in love. Then, to her horror, she discovers that her lover is already engaged to a woman of a higher social class. Certain that she has been used, she goes mad. Her lover is filled with guilt, but that doesn't keep vengeful evil spirits from pursuing him. Giselle dies and returns as a ghost to protect her lover from the evil spirits. In the Dance Theater of Harlem production, the story remained the same, but the locale became the Louisiana bayous of the nineteenth century and Giselle became the favorite mistress of one of Louisiana's nineteenth-century planta-

For Dance Theater of Harlem, Arthur Mitchell chose some classical
ballet works choreographed by George Balanchine, the great choreographer who had hired Mitchell for the American Ballet Theater. *Martha
Swope.*

148

tion owners. There were new costumes and settings, but the choreography was basically unchanged. The company used expressive movement to carry the story along, and made the audiences feel the joy and tragedy of the story.

Introduced as *Creole Giselle* in 1984 at the London Coliseum, it became the first American ballet to win the Laurence Olivier Award as best new dance production of the year. The troupe included the production in its spring 1987 season in New York. "What a wonderful production," wrote Jack Anderson of *The New York Times*, after seeing it at Davis Hall at the City University of New York in March 1987.

The following month, DTH presented a program of six works by George Balanchine, who had hired Arthur Mitchell at the New York City Ballet. That same season they did a production of Jerome Robbins' *Fancy Free*, a musical comedy classic, and a "work in progress" called *Phoenix Rising*, which was jointly choreographed by Arthur Mitchell and Billy Wilson (a former dancer on Broadway, member of the National Ballet of Holland, and choreographer for the Broadway musical *Bubblin' Brown Sugar*), and with sets and costumes designed by Geoffrey Holder.

In the 1980s, *Firebird*, created for Diaghilev's Ballets Russes at the turn of the century, became closely identified with DTH, and in 1988, its twentieth year, the company toured for the first time in the land from which *Firebird* and many other great ballets had originated. They took with them a brand-new dance choreographed by Mitchell called *John Henry*, based on the folk hero who was said to be so strong that with his sledgehammer and steel bit

149

he could tunnel the way for more miles of railroad track than a steam drill. It was the first ballet that Mitchell had choreographed himself in thirteen years, for so much of his time had been taken up by administrative duties and fund-raising.

The five-week Russian tour was a great success. "We played to over six thousand people a night," said Mitchell. "People were sitting on floors and in the aisles. People scaled the walls of the theater in Tbilisi trying to get in."

Since the middle 1980s, DTH has been on the road for up to thirty weeks each year, not just to earn recognition but to stay alive financially. Over half their annual budget of six million dollars is earned through performing.

It was extremely expensive to fund the school and the company—just the electricity bill for the DTH building was over three thousand dollars a month. In 1986, a fire all but destroyed the building on West 152nd Street, forcing Mitchell to divert the company's already strained resources into renovation. It would have been the perfect opportunity for Mitchell to move downtown, but he was, and is, committed to remaining in Harlem to serve as an example to other urban black areas. Thus far, however, no individual has shown the vision or commitment that Mitchell has.

For the same reason, Mitchell has no intention of integrating his dance company anytime soon. While the school is integrated, the company is all black. Mitchell feels it is important to train and give experience to black dancers. When asked when he is going to integrate the company, he says, "As soon as other major companies across the country really start integrating and accepting blacks and other minorities."

While he is realistic about the problems that still confront blacks in ballet, Mitchell nevertheless is optimistic about the future, especially that of his own company. He started DTH because he wanted to help black youngsters in the best way he knew, through his art. Twenty years later, he believes he has accomplished his dream.

The company has a ritual in which they form a circle, holding hands, before each company class. They call it the Circle of Strength. One dancer says a few words for the entire company. Mitchell remembers well the last class in the Soviet Union, during the company's 1988 trip there. It was Donald Williams' turn to speak, but instead of talking he sang "I Believe." Tears came to Mitchell's eyes: "I couldn't teach," he said later. "I sat down and watched." Referring to the barriers he'd had to surmount to start DTH and keep it going, he said, "And they said it couldn't be done. I can say for myself, I was so proud. I say to myself, 'Arthur, a job well done.' "

Unlike comparable white ballet companies such as the Joffrey Ballet and the Eliot Feld Ballet Company, DTH still does not have a regular New York concert season at a major midtown theater.

Chapter 7
Integration and Innovation: Black Dance Matures in the 1960s

While Arthur Mitchell and others led the way for black dancers in classical dance, many black dancers were pursuing different avenues in popular and modern dance. In the area of popular dance, there had not been a real, single-dance craze in the United States since the Jitterbug of the 1940s. Although popular dancing had returned with rock 'n' roll, and there were a number of rock 'n' roll dances that nearly all teenagers did, few stood out from the others, and fewer appealed to adults. In 1960, however, a single-dance craze swept the nation.

The Twist

Hank Ballard had composed and recorded a song called "The Twist" in the middle 1950s, but it was not a huge

In 1960, a recording of "The Twist" by a young Philadelphian named Ernest "Chubby Checker" Evans launched a dance craze that swept the country. *AP/Wide World Photos.*

sensation. A few years later, an overweight young black man named Chubby Checker recorded it and performed it on Clay Cole's TV show, and suddenly America went crazy over the new dance.

Chubby Checker's real name was Ernest Evans, and he was born in 1941 in Philadelphia. During high school, he held a part-time job as a chicken plucker at a poultry shop, and he would entertain the customers with songs and jokes. The manager of the shop thought he was so talented that he introduced him to Kal Mann of Parkway Records, and when he was just eighteen, Ernest was signed to a contract with Parkway. It was then that he took the professional name Chubby, because he admired the singer Fats Domino and because that was the nickname his friends called him. His first record, "The Class," released in early 1959, was fairly successful. It landed him a spot on *American Bandstand*, and after seeing him perform, and hearing that he liked Fats Domino, Dick Clark's wife suggested that he call himself Chubby Checker. It was as Chubby Checker that he recorded the song that would bring him worldwide fame.

Kal Mann of Parkway records saw the teenagers on *American Bandstand* dancing to Hank Ballard's record, "The Twist," twisting their bodies by moving their arms from left to right quickly, partners dancing face to face but never touching. He saw that they enjoyed the dance and decided that Chubby Checker could do a better job with the song. It was a brilliant idea. "The Twist" was the number one popular song in 1960 and again in 1961, the only song in history to hit number one on the national charts two different times.

Adults picked up the dance, too, and started looking around for someone to give them Twist lessons. Arthur Murray, known for his ballroom dancing studios, offered "6 Easy Lessons for $25." New dance places called discotheques (where records—discs—rather than live musicians often supplied the music) had opened to take advantage of the new interest in popular dancing, so now there were places to go to dance the Twist. The first discotheque was the Whiskey a Go Go in Los Angeles, which opened in 1961. One of the most famous was the Peppermint Lounge in New York, and in fact, a group called Joey Dee and the Starlighters recorded a song called "The Peppermint Twist." By 1962, America was "Twistin' the Night Away," to quote the title of a popular Sam Cooke song. And in 1962, the Motown group the Marvelettes followed their big hit "Please, Mr. Postman," with "Twistin' Postman."

Chubby Checker made several more Twist records. He also introduced other new dances, like the Hucklebuck, the Pony, and the Fly. The Pony, at least, harked back to the Slow Drag, which originated in New Orleans in the late nineteenth century, where it was danced by couples close together, with sensual hip movements.

A raft of new dances followed the Twist. They included the Monkey, the Bug, the Frug, the Hitchhike, the Watusi, the Jerk, the Hully-Gully, the Boogaloo. Some of these also could be traced back to the old Shimmy (the Frug) or the old Heebie-Jeebies (the Bug and the Monkey). Others were simply pantomimes with a little extra body movement and footwork. None was as successful as the Twist, which, like all the most popular dances, is still done on occasion.

Soon, white teenagers and adults were doing the Twist in trendy new discotheques such as the Peppermint Lounge in New York City. *AP/Wide World Photos.*

By 1964, the Twist had found its way into the choreography of at least one modern dance master, Alvin Ailey. Ailey's use of the Twist exemplifies one advantage of modern dance over ballet. Modern dance allows for much greater experimentation in new forms, and the latest dance craze was just as appropriate for adaptation as a political movement such as the civil rights struggle.

By the time World War II ended, modern dance had been fully accepted in the United States and had influenced ballet, just as ballet had influenced modern dance. Most modern dancers and modern dance choreographers now had ballet training, giving their movements a lightness and quickness that earlier modern dancers had not possessed. By the same token, ballet dancers had usually taken some modern dance, and they now were not so rigid about the position of the torso, realizing that there were certain advantages, among them gracefulness, to a flexible upper body. Since there was plenty of room for both types of dancing, a healthy give-and-take existed between them.

As for black modern dance, some critics have stated that it should be called jazz dance and that it was easy to distinguish dances choreographed by black choreographers because of a "strong rhythmic impulse and an alert, bouncy carriage to the body," as Don McDonagh stated in *The Complete Guide to Modern Dance*. Whether or not this is in fact the case, there is no question that black modern dance, and modern dancers, were integrated into mainstream modern dance by the middle 1950s and that many modern dance companies, whether headed by blacks or by whites, were integrated.

157

Donald McKayle

Donald McKayle was born in New York City on July 6, 1930, and first became excited about modern dance after he saw a performance by Pearl Primus. After graduating from high school, he enrolled at the City College of the City University of New York, but he also followed in Primus' footsteps by winning a year's scholarship to the New Dance Group. There, he studied with Primus, Sophie Maslow, Jean Erdman, and others. He made his professional debut at the Mansfield Theater in the spring of 1948, in dances choreographed by Maslow and Erdman.

He performed in New Dance Group concerts and choreographed his first works when only eighteen—*Exodus*, *Saturday's Child*, and *Creole Afternoon*. He also danced as guest artist with other troupes, and met other choreographers, among them Daniel Nagrin. Nagrin was assistant choreographer to Helen Tamiris in the musical comedy *God Bless You All* (1950), in which McKayle had one of his first opportunities to dance in a show. Together with other choreographers, McKayle and Nagrin formed the Contemporary Dance Group, and in May 1951, they presented a concert at Hunter College at which McKayle's now-classic piece *Games* was first performed.

"It was a childhood memory that triggered [*Games*]," McKayle wrote in the 1960s. "It was dusk, and the block was dimly lit by a street lamp around which we hovered choosing a game. The street, playground of tenement children, was soon ringing with calls and cries, the happy

Donald McKayle's *Games* (1951) has become a classic. In 1986, it was featured at the American Dance Festival. *Jay Anderson photo, American Dance Festival.*

159

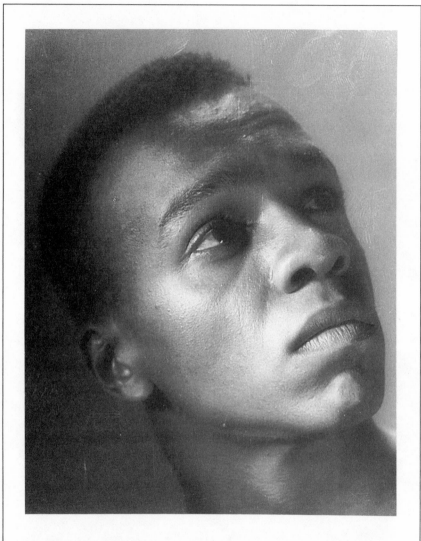

Donald McKayle began his career as a dancer but soon turned to choreography as well. In the history of black dance, he is best known for his choreographic works. *Museum of the City of New York.*

shouts of the young." In the work, McKayle did not use children, or even particularly young-looking dancers, but somehow he captured the feelings and imaginations and fears of children in the piece.

Unfortunately, the Contemporary Dance Group was not financially successful. McKayle continued to choreograph, however. In 1952, he developed *Her Name Was Harriet* (about the famous Underground Railroad conductor Harriet Tubman), and in 1953, a piece called *Nocturne*. In 1954, he danced in *House of Flowers*, in which Geoffrey Holder and Carmen De Lavallade made their debuts. Meanwhile, he had won a scholarship to the Martha Graham School of Dance, and he performed with her company on their Far Eastern tour in 1955–1956.

In 1959, McKayle choreographed another classic work, *Rainbow 'Round My Shoulder*, inspired by the music and rhythms of Southern black chain gangs. He assembled a group to perform it that included Charles Moore and Mary Hinkson, and it was later adopted as part of the repertory of the Alvin Ailey Dance Theatre. Almost as popular was *District Storyville*, about the development of jazz in New Orleans, which McKayle created in 1962 and which also became part of the Ailey repertory.

Important works of the 1970s included *Barrio*, *Songs of the Disinherited*, *Migrations*, *Sojourn*, and *Autumn Leaves*. A London critic wrote in 1967 that McKayle's best works dealt "not with abstractions but with people; living, laughing, suffering, bitter, pitiful, protesting, superbly human beings." That remained true of McKayle's best later works as well.

161

McKayle had a company in New York for a while in the early 1960s, and performed both in New York and in Europe, but he never tried to maintain a permanent company. Rather, when he had a particular work, or a specific season in which he wanted his works performed, he assembled a group as the need arose.

McKayle was one of the first black modern dancers/choreographers to do extensive work in television. Beginning in 1963, he choreographed TV specials at the rate of about one a year, including *The Bill Cosby Special* in 1968 and a series of segments for *The Ed Sullivan Show* in 1966–1967. He choreographed the dances for the 1970 Oscar presentations, the Marlo Thomas special *Free to Be . . . You and Me*, and the pilot for the CBS sitcom *Good Times*. He also staged dances for films, including two Walt Disney movies—*Bedknobs and Broomsticks* and *Charlie and the Angel*—and for the film biography of the heavyweight boxing champion Jack Johnson, *The Great White Hope*.

On Broadway, he choreographed dances for *Golden Boy* (1964), *I'm Solomon* (1969), *Raisin* (a musical based on *A Raisin in the Sun*, 1974), and *Dr. Jazz* (1975). In 1980, he directed and choreographed the show *Sophisticated Ladies*, based on the music of Duke Ellington, but by the time it opened on Broadway, he had left the show due to artistic and personality differences with one of its stars, Gregory Hines. He also staged cabaret and nightclub acts for many singers, including Harry Belafonte. In between, he taught dance and choreography at the New Dance Group in New York, at Bennington College in Vermont, in Tel Aviv, in Cologne, Germany, and in London. He was one of the founders of the Inner City Cultural Center in Los Angeles in the 1970s.

One reason Donald McKayle has worked in so many fields has been the basic need to support himself. But in doing so, he has touched the lives of many young black dancers and has had a major impact both on them as individuals and on black modern dance in general. In fact, it has been his fate to advance the careers of other dancers more than he has advanced his own. Unlike Arthur Mitchell and Alvin Ailey, McKayle never became a star. But he helped many dancers who would become stars.

Alvin Ailey

As important as McKayle, indeed, if not more important to modern dance in general, and black modern dance in particular, is Alvin Ailey. Not only has he distinguished himself as an individual dancer/choreographer, he has also accomplished the rare feat of keeping a permanent company together almost continuously for some thirty years.

Ailey was born in January 1931, in Rogers, Texas, into grinding poverty. His seventeen-year-old mother was so undernourished that she was unable to nurse him. His parents separated when he was young, and Alvin was a lonely child who began to write poetry at an early age. He also learned early about the sharp divisions between blacks and whites in Texas, and when in 1942 he moved with his mother to Los Angeles, he pleaded with her not to send him to an integrated school. He eventually adjusted

163

to being around whites, but even then, he had a strong sense of "his people." As a teenager, he was active in sports. He also took tap and primitive dance lessons, but he did not take dancing seriously. On graduation from high school in 1948, he briefly enrolled at the University of California at Los Angeles before transferring to Los Angeles City College. His plan was to become a teacher.

In 1949, he was introduced to the work of Lester Horton. Ailey was attracted to the Horton technique of modern dance and by the theatricality that Horton stressed. No doubt he was also attracted by the fact that Horton's was the first integrated modern dance company and that the pieces it performed were often ethnic pieces, since Horton had a keen interest in Native American culture. For a time, he wavered between a career in dance and a more stable career as a teacher.

With the help of a scholarship, he took composition and technique classes with Horton. He also worked in the stage crew and danced with the Lester Horton Dance Theatre. But in 1951, he decided that he needed a steady career and transferred to San Francisco State College to major in Romance languages so he could teach them. While at San Francisco State, he began to dance with a nightclub act that traveled around the state, and by the time the group reached Los Angeles, he had changed his mind and decided that a dance career was for him, no matter how unstable it was. He rejoined the Lester Horton Dance Theatre.

Just a few months later, Lester Horton died. The company wished to remain together and decided to have a go at it. Ailey got the opportunity to choreograph for the

164

company, and in 1954, his works *Mourning Mourning* and *According to St. Francis* were performed by the Horton company in Los Angeles and at the Jacob's Pillow Dance Festival near Lee, Massachusetts, which was directed by modern dance pioneer Ted Shawn. During that same year, Ailey also choreographed Darius Milhaud's *Creation of the World* for the Horton company's performance with the San Diego Symphony and danced in the Hollywood film *Carmen Jones*, which was released by Twentieth-Century Fox in 1955.

In addition to choreographing for the Horton company, Ailey taught at the Lester Horton School and directed the Horton Children's Theatre. But when he was invited, with fellow Horton dancer Carmen De Lavallade, to appear in *House of Flowers* on Broadway in 1954, he jumped at the opportunity to go to New York.

During his first years in New York City, Ailey studied with Martha Graham, Doris Humphrey, Anna Sokolow, and others. He also studied ballet under Karel Shook. Meanwhile, he danced in several musical shows, including *The Carefree Tree* (1955) and Harry Belafonte's *Sing, Man, Sing* (1956). In 1957, he was lead dancer in *Jamaica*, starring Lena Horne and Ricardo Montalban, and the following spring, with fellow dancer Richard Parham, he assembled a group of dancers who were mostly from the cast of the show and presented a program at the 92nd Street YMHA, with Talley Beatty as guest artist. For that program, Ailey choreographed *Ode and Homage* (to Lester Horton), *Blues Suite*, and a group of five dances with Latin themes that was later titled *Cinco Latinos*.

Based on the success of that program, Ailey decided

to take the bold step of forming his own dance company. It was fitting that the Alvin Ailey American Dance Theatre gave its first full-scale concerts in December 1958 at the Y where they had made their first appearance. It was also appropriate that Carmen De Lavallade was guest artist. She would dance often with the company over the next few years, and serve as co-director in 1962.

In January 1960, the Alvin Ailey company premiered what has been called Ailey's masterwork, *Revelations*, at the 92nd Street Y. The program notes state that it is a suite exploring the "motivations and emotions of American Negro religious music." Others have called it a hymn to God and man. It was Ailey's interpretation of American spirituals, and the sets and costumes echoed Southern nineteenth-century life. In one scene, weeping willow branches serve as a canopy over women in long, ruffled dresses carrying parasols, and bare-torsoed men in white trousers. In the tradition of the Cakewalk, the women don wide-brimmed hats and the men wear starched shirts and vests. The choreography reflects the moods of the spirituals—a longing for deliverance in "Didn't My Lord Deliver Daniel," and soul-stamping joy in "Rocka My Soul." Audiences responded to it with tumultuous applause, and for the next several years, no Ailey program was complete without it. In fact, it is a perennial favorite in the Ailey repertory, and when performed in December 1988, twenty-nine years after its premier, it received rousing applause from audiences and rave reviews from critics.

By the fall of 1960, the Alvin Ailey American Dance Theatre had a home at the Clark Center for the Performing Arts, part of the West Side YMCA. Using this base, Ailey

Alvin Ailey, shown here in the 1950s, began his career as a dancer whose work strongly emphasized black themes. *Museum of the City of New York.*

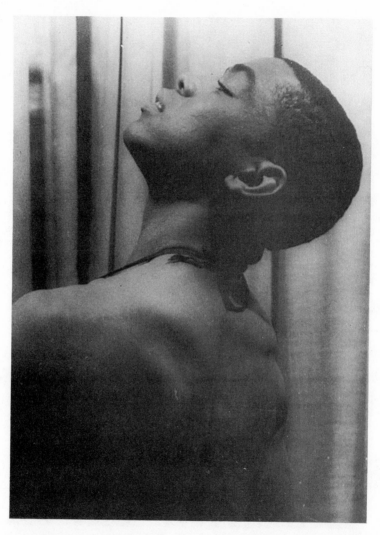

A portrait of Alvin Ailey at the beginning of his professional dance career. *Museum of the City of New York.*

adopted a procedure that was highly unusual in modern dance: using the work of other choreographers in his repertory. The first instance was a revival of Lester Horton's *The Beloved* for Carmen De Lavallade. He also presented the New York premiere of John Butler's *Portrait of Billie*, about the tragic jazz singer Billie Holiday, and which was also danced by Carmen De Lavallade. Ailey himself danced solo to Samuel Barber's *Hermit Songs*. One of the most successful of his own choreographed works of that period was *Roots of the Blues*, a duet danced by Ailey and De Lavallade.

De Lavallade served as co-director of the Alvin Ailey Dance Theatre when it became the first black American company to perform in Southeast Asia in a thirteen-week tour sponsored by the U.S. State Department. The tour was hugely successful and established the international appeal of the company, which would later go on other extended engagements abroad.

It was after that tour that Alvin Ailey integrated his company, explaining, "I thought that we were being put into a category—I wanted my dancers to feel that they were not just 'black dancers,' that they were part of society." Integration was still a goal of most blacks in 1962, but in just a few years, many would turn toward black nationalism and separatism instead, and Ailey "got a lot of flack" about having an integrated company. He refused to change, however, feeling that "an integrated company enlarges the statement I've been trying to make."

By means of his integrated company, Ailey has broken down many racial barriers and stereotypes about dancing and race. He has shown that white dancers can dance the blues, that Japanese dancers can execute jazz technique, and that black dancers can dance a classic ballet such as *Swan Lake*.

His company is also different from many other modern dance groups in that a particular body type does not predominate. Although this sometimes diminishes the ensemble work of the company, Ailey prefers hiring individuals to types. "I've always felt that I wanted to celebrate the differences in people," Ailey has explained. "I didn't want all the same bodies, or all the same color, in my company."

During the summer of 1962, Ailey was one of several choreographers invited to the Rhode Island estate of Mrs. Rebekah Harkness, who was then supporting the Robert Joffrey Ballet. Mrs. Harkness wanted new dances created for the Joffrey, and in a workshop arrangement Ailey created several important pieces, including *Feast of Ashes*, which later became part of the repertory of the Harkness Ballet.

Throughout the middle 1960s, the Alvin Ailey American Dance Theatre toured nationally and internationally, participating in all the major dance festivals. Its most acclaimed program at that time was called *Three for Now*, a jazz suite made up of *Gillespiana: Reflections in D*, a tribute to Dizzy Gillespie danced solo by Ailey to music by Duke Ellington; James Truitte's *Variations*, a tribute to Lester Horton; and *Light!*, a composite of jazz styles from the Suzy-Q to the Twist.

In 1964, the company undertook its first European tour, creating such a stir that in Hamburg, Germany, they had sixty-one curtain calls. The dynamic, expressive dancing of the company and the rich repertory reflected both the technical skill and commitment of the dancers and the restless, forceful energy of Ailey himself. Ailey, who was thirty-three by that time, stopped dancing when that tour ended and turned over his roles to other men in the company. That same year, he was one of eight choreographers awarded major grants by the National Council on the Arts. The popularity of the company was undiminished, and they continued touring nationally and internationally; in April 1966, they were the only integrated modern dance company to appear at the World Festival of Negro Arts in Dakar, Senegal. But that was also a time when the company was in severe financial straits and Ailey had to disband it for about a year.

Once he had raised more money and re-formed his company, Ailey continued to use the work of other choreographers. The repertory for a European tour in 1967 included Geoffrey Holder's *Prodigal Son* and Paul Sanasardo's *Metallics*. That same year the troupe, again under the auspices of the U.S. State Department, toured Israel and nine African countries.

While the company was very successful, relative to other modern dance companies, Ailey faced unrelenting creative and financial pressures. Keeping the company fresh took a great deal of work. Ailey had to keep coming up with new dances, and so he frequently turned to the work of other choreographers. It also took a great deal of money to maintain a dance company. More than once, the existence of the company was saved only by emergency grants from various Federal arts funding agencies or private gifts.

171

More than once, it was the U.S. State Department that kept the company going by sending it on international tours (Russia and Eastern and Western Europe in 1970–71). "We toured yearly and fell apart yearly," Ailey is fond of saying, adding that the company was consistently more acclaimed in Europe than in the United States and citing racism as the reason.

Ailey was delighted when the troupe was offered a permanent home at the Brooklyn Academy of Music in 1969, where they remained until 1971, when they became one of a family of dance troupes that called City Center in Manhattan home.

By the time the Alvin Ailey Dance Theatre moved over to City Center, Ailey had begun to depart from the concrete imagery of his story dances and to use more ballet technique and create more plotless works, like *Streams* (1970), which he created for his own company, and *The River* (also 1970), which he choreographed for the American Ballet Theatre to music by Duke Ellington.

Two years later, he had decided that modern dance companies should do repertory the way classical ballet companies do: revive older works so that they are not lost. Over the next few years, his company staged Donald McKayle's *Rainbow 'Round My Shoulder*, Katherine Dunham's *Choros*, and works by Pearl Primus, José Limón, Talley Beatty, and Ted Shawn.

By the 1980s, the Alvin Ailey American Dance Theatre was no longer resident at City Center, although it continued to perform there annually. Instead, it appeared for brief seasons at a variety of different theaters, including

Lincoln Center. In 1984, it became the first mostly black modern dance company to perform a two-week season at the Metropolitan Opera House. It was also only the second modern dance group to perform there, the first having been Martha Graham's company. Instead of performing to taped music, the troupe was able to dance to live music provided by the resident orchestra, which was a great pleasure for the dancers. Ailey chose to premiere his new work, *Precipice*, at the Metropolitan, because its stage was perfect for the ambitious work, which included twenty-six characters, fifty-six costumes, and two backdrops on loan from the company of the Paris Opéra. Two guest dancers from the Paris Opéra company danced at the Met for the occasion.

In 1988, the Ailey company devoted much of its repertory to a tribute to Katherine Dunham, reconstructing historical dances that she choreographed back in the 1930s and 1940s. Thanks to a major grant from the Ford Foundation that made the project possible, they also renovated and restored the original costumes and set designs by Dunham's husband, John Pratt. Katherine Dunham herself served as a consultant on the project, teaching the Ailey dancers the Dunham technique, particularly the use of the pelvis.

For the 1988–1989 season, the Ailey company went back to a varied repertory that included *Survivors*, a social-protest work that featured tributes to the South African freedom fighters Nelson and Winnie Mandela. The backdrop is a large hanging sculpture with bars suggesting a jail cell. Dudley Williams, as Nelson Mandela, is behind those bars. Sharrell Mesh, as Winnie Mandela, screams

173

silently in rage. The two engage in a tender love duet through the bars. Other dancers, playing ordinary black South Africans, emerge from the shadows to pay tribute to the couple who symbolize the fight against apartheid.

Later in the season, four pieces premiered in New York: Ailey's *Opus*, Donald Byrd's *Shards*, Kelvin Rotardier's *Tell It Like It Is*, and Rovan Deon's *From the Mountains*. They also staged revivals of Ailey's *Streams* and *Masakela Language*, choreographed to the music of the African musician Hugh Masakela.

In 1987, at the American Dance Festival in Durham, North Carolina, Ailey received the Scripps Dance Award, a prestigious award given for lifetime contributions to American modern dance, including $25,000, the largest annual prize offered in the performing arts. In announcing the award, Charles Reinhart, director of the festival, said, "Alvin Ailey's remarkable contribution to modern dance continues to make a significant impact on the field. The language of his choreography, informed by the black experience, is universal in its appeal. Mr. Ailey has achieved a distinctive place in our culture." In accepting the prize, Ailey said, "I am part of Isadora Duncan. I am part of Martha Graham. I am part of Doris Humphrey. I am part of Asadata Dafora. And I am part of Lester Horton, who made a boy, an eighteen-year-old athlete in sweat pants, feel important."

Alvin Ailey died on December 1, 1989 in New York City. Ailey had a profound impact on a whole generation of young dancers. The members of his company gained experience in all sorts of techniques and in the work of dozens of choreographers. Perhaps the most famous member, after Carmen De Lavallade, is Judith Jamison, one of the few well-known black women in modern dance.

Judith Jamison

It is not surprising that two of the most famous early pioneers of black modern dance were women—Katherine Dunham and Pearl Primus. The larger American public has traditionally found it easier to accept black women in most areas because they are somehow less threatening than black men. But in more recent times, the big names in black modern dance, and particularly in black modern dance choreography, have been men. Judith Jamison is an exception. She is a star who had a long career as a dancer and then moved into choreography.

Jamison (the first syllable of her last name is pronounced like jam in jam session) was born in Philadelphia, Pennsylvania, on May 10, 1944. She began dancing at the age of six at the Judimar School of Dance and made her stage debut at Town Hall in Philadelphia that same year. She later studied with other teachers, including Antony Tudor and Maria Swoboda. Her training was principally in ballet. She was an athlete in school, and on graduation from high school, she went on a physical education scholarship to Fisk University in Nashville, Tennessee. There, she majored in psychology and studied for three semesters before she decided that her heart was in the dance.

She returned to Philadelphia and enrolled in the Philadelphia Dance Academy. She made her formal debut in 1959 as Myrtha in *Giselle*. In 1964, while she was still studying at the Philadelphia Dance Academy, she was discovered by the great choreographer Agnes de Mille (who had created the dances for the show *Oklahoma!* in 1943 and almost single-handedly changed the whole concept of musical-theater dancing). De Mille took Jamison to New York to dance with three other black dancers in *The Four Marys*.

The following year, the American Ballet Theatre engaged all four black dancers from *The Four Marys* for its spring 1965 season. Jamison took advantage of the opportunity to take classes at the American Ballet Theatre and took every class she could, almost always the only black student. She didn't mind, however, since she had gone to predominantly white schools in Philadelphia. Unfortunately, when the season ended, so did the ABT's lease of the New York State Theater and its contract with the four black dancers. It did not renew any of the contracts.

Jamison remained in New York, hoping to get another dancing job. When she ran out of money, Carmen De Lavallade, who had also danced with the ABT that season, let her sleep on her couch. De Lavallade told her to be patient, that it took time; but Jamison couldn't help thinking that if she were as lithe, beautiful, and light-complected as De Lavallade, she wouldn't be having so much trouble. She was dark-skinned. Moreover, she was big, athletic, with exceptionally long arms. And she was tall—five foot eleven inches—and could rise to six foot five inches *en*

176

pointe. She knew that she was different, and wondered if that would prevent her from pursuing her career in dance.

At one point, she took a job at the 1964–1965 World's Fair in Flushing Meadow Park, operating the Log Flume Ride. Just when she was about to despair about continuing her dance career, she got the chance to audition for Donald McKayle at the Choreographer's Workshop on East 51st Street in Manhattan. It was a typical cattle-call audition, and hundreds of young hopefuls showed up. The first task was to separate out the most likely talents, and McKayle's assistant for the audition, Paula Kelly, had that task. She launched into a few routines that she expected the young dancers to follow, and Jamison was flabbergasted. She had never danced like that, and didn't think she could do so now. She tried gamely, but she was cut after the first round. Hurrying from the stage, she stumbled and almost fell over a man sitting on the steps of the stage.

Over the next few days, Jamison decided to face the reality that she was never going to make it in New York. She had almost made up her mind to return to Philadelphia when she got a call from Alvin Ailey inviting her to join his company. He had been the man sitting on the steps, over whom she had almost fallen, at the McKayle audition. He was also a good friend of Carmen De Lavallade, who had prevailed upon him to give Jamison a try.

Judith Jamison made her debut with the Ailey company on November 30, 1965, in Chicago, not in an Ailey work but as one of the corps in Talley Beatty's *Congo Tango Palace*. The company did six weeks of one-night stands.

177

Her first performances with the company in New York were in "House of the Rising Sun," in Ailey's *Blues Suite*; in his *Revelations*; and in Beatty's *The Road of the Phoebe Snow*, in which she appeared as one of a quartet. On February 14, 1966, the Ailey company began its third, and Judith Jamison her first, European tour. "We opened the European tour in Muenster [Germany] and that night I realized the kind of status the company had in Europe," Jamison later recalled. "The audience applauded for *one— solid—hour!* That made the audiences at home seem pretty tepid."

It was also during this tour, however, that financial problems caused Ailey to disband the company. Jamison and her boyfriend, dancer Miguel Godreau, were taken into the Harkness Ballet in Paris and later accompanied the troupe to its home in Watch Hill, Rhode Island, at the estate of Mrs. Rebekah Harkness. There, however, Godreau quit the troupe, feeling that the Harkness Ballet could not benefit his career, which was primarily in modern dance. Jamison, by contrast, felt very comfortable in ballet and believed that her time with the Ailey group had been just a detour. Her romance with Godreau continued, off and on. They were married in 1972, but the marriage was annulled two years later.

For Jamison, one of the best things about being with the Harkness Ballet was the opportunity to study at the school with the eminent ballerina Patricia Wilde. Dancing with the Harkness troupe was another matter. Jamison was considered unsuited to most of the repertory, which was heavy on "tutu ballets," so called because of the little net skirt that ballerinas traditionally wear. She ended up

Too tall, dark-skinned, and athletic for classical ballet, Judith Jamison found her niche in modern dance and became one of the most famous members of the Alvin Ailey troupe. *Museum of the City of New York.*

being cast in two ballets choreographed by Alvin Ailey for the company, *Yemanja* and *Ariadne*, neither of which was well received by critics, who hardly mentioned Judith's dancing. She was also lonely. "Everyone at Harkness was nice to me but I had no close friends," she said later. "I found out what it means to be a black dancer in a white company." And then, if all that had not been enough, she injured her foot.

The Harkness Ballet was dancing in Mrs. Harkness' hometown of St. Louis, Missouri, at the Kiel Auditorium. The stage was slippery, and in the course of doing four successive pirouettes she fell. The doctor she was sent to told her that she had sprained her foot and that she could still dance, but not for a while. She left the tour and returned to New York.

She had been in New York only a few days when Alvin Ailey called to tell her he was reactivating the company and told her to "come home." Joyfully, she rejoined Ailey, and worked hard for the next four years to establish herself in the company. From 1971 until her retirement in the middle 1980s, she occupied a position comparable to that of a prima ballerina in a classical company. She danced an extensive range of the Ailey company's repertory and in many works choreographed for her, of which the most famous is Ailey's great solo *Cry*.

Ailey dedicated *Cry* to "all black women everywhere— especially our mothers," and it was about the stages in a woman's life and the stages of black life in white society. Jamison began the dance wearing a long white dress, her head wrapped in a cloth. She unwound the cloth and

180

used it to wash the floor, portraying a slave or a domestic, or merely someone who is oppressed. She lifted up her arms in a silent call for freedom. Then she sank back to the ground, as if in great pain. She fought her way back up, her head swinging around and around as if to create an invisible shield around her. Finally, she rose up to her full height, then stood on tiptoe and extended her arms and lifted her head high, having triumphed over all the pain that life had dealt her.

It was a powerful dance, and especially powerful when danced by Jamison. Often, faces in the audience were wet with tears when the curtain came down, and sometimes Jamison was crying, too. In her rendition of *Cry*, the dance was not just about black women, but about anyone who had ever been oppressed. She danced with such fury, with such "terrible splendor," as one writer put it, that her body ached with tension and sweat streamed down her skin.

During the 1970s, Judith Jamison achieved the status of an international star, not only as principal dancer with the Ailey company but also by virtue of many appearances as guest artist with European companies, including the Hamburg Ballet and the ballet of the Vienna State Opera. Her height, the length and extension of her arms, the strength of her long legs—all the qualities that had prevented her from being successful in classical ballet—were the perfect qualities for the energetic, emotional, restless modern dance choreography that Ailey favored and that was gaining popularity in Europe. In 1972, she and Anthony Dowell, premier dancer with England's Royal Ballet,

181

were recipients of the Dance Magazine Award. Katherine Dunham presented Jamison's award to her. That same year, she was selected by President Richard Nixon to serve on the board of the National Endowment for the Arts. She served on the board until 1976.

In 1980, Jamison assumed the position of co-director of the Ailey company for its seventeenth season and a Japanese tour. In 1981, she took a leave of absence to star in the Broadway musical *Sophisticated Ladies*, based on the music of Duke Ellington.

While Judith Jamison did not pursue a career in the classical ballet, she did prove that a woman of her color and size could exhibit just as much grace as a smaller woman of lighter complexion. She was a unique dancer, with a power comparable to that of Pearl Primus. She now devotes most of her time to encouraging young black dancers and to choreographing works of her own.

She created her first work, *Divining*, in 1984 for a student workshop at the Ailey school. After that, she was invited to choreograph other works, including one for students at the University of the Arts in Philadelphia, her hometown, where she later became a visiting distinguished professor. In 1988, she formed The Jamison Project, a company of young dancers. In November 1988, this group appeared at the Joyce Theater in New York in a program featuring *Divining*, *Time Out*, and *Tease*, all choreographed by Jamison. In that same program, she danced a solo created for her by Garth Fagan, founder of the Bucket Dance Theater. Called "Scene Seen," it was tailored to her gifts as a mature performer with less power but more subtlety of movement.

After Alvin Ailey's death in December 1989, Judith Jamison was chosen to become the new director of the Alvin Ailey American Dance Theatre.

Alvin Ailey also influenced a whole generation of dancers who have not necessarily worked with him. Among them is Kevin Jeff, a native of Brooklyn, who formed an all-black modern dance company, based in Brooklyn, in 1981. Before that, this graduate of Manhattan's High School of the Performing Arts had had a highly successful, though brief, career on Broadway, playing the role of the Winged Monkey in *The Wiz* and dancing in the show *Comin' Uptown*, starring Gregory Hines. He had auditioned for a part in the Jewish musical *Fiddler on the Roof* but was turned down "because he hadn't lived the experience."

He quit Broadway in 1981 at the age of twenty-two to start his own modern dance company, Jeff's Jubilation! Dance Company. While admitting to being influenced by Ailey, he points out several major differences. One is that he has thus far refused to accept grant money from arts organizations, even though that means he hasn't been able to increase the size of his company beyond ten dancers. Another is that his troupe is all black and he does not care to integrate it, feeling that a dancer must "live the experience" of being black in order to dance African and African-influenced dances. The dances he choreographs are a mixture of jazz, modern, ballet, and traditional African dance; for example, he combines an African head roll with a classical arabesque. "The African movement is the glue that links together the ballet, modern, and jazz," he says. "It's dynamic and healing. It requires a lot of stamina, but it's subtle. It has a lot of impact as theater."

Another black modern dance company is the Black Pearl Dance Company, founded in the Bronx, New York, in 1981, by dancer and choreographer Maria Mitchell. It is unique among the city's many dance companies because it is devoted to the preservation of black literature through dance theater. Among its major works has been *Circles*, based on the works of Langston Hughes, Zora Neale Hurston, and the Reverend Martin Luther King, Jr., which premiered in 1986. In 1987, the company's program was called *A House Divided* and was based on a short story by Alice Walker and on Donald Woods' *Biko* and *The Children Under Apartheid*. The Black Pearl Dance Company is also unique in that it often uses children and guest artists to augment its six-member core.

There are too many different companies across the United States to mention them all here. But this great variety also ensures a great vitality in modern dance— and not just black modern dance, but white modern dance as well.

Chapter 8
The Current Era: A Fine Variety

Popular dance fads seem to occur about every ten years, and the decades of the 1970s and 1980s each had its craze. These fads often drew on African dance movements, and in the 1970s, the rage was the heavily Latin-influenced disco dancing. Disco music combined the pulsating, funky beat of sixties soul music with a stylish, slick tempo, and the complex, sinuous rhythms of Latin dance music. The luxurious orchestrations of disco music emphasized strings, brass, and percussion. Van McCoy's recording of "The Hustle," released in 1975, popularized disco, as did the movie *Saturday Night Fever*, starring John Travolta.

Disco dancing was much like ballroom dancing but to a heavy, fast, and repetitive beat (the standard disco tempo was 150 beats per minute). While the Twist was danced without touching, disco dancing was real contact dancing.

In the 1980s, break dancing became the newest national dance craze, although the average American had sense enough not to try the risky acrobatic stunts of "street break dancers." *AP/Wide World Photo.*

Steps from Latin dances like the Samba were added, as well as acrobatics. Couples vied with each other to do the most intricate dance-acrobatic routines. At first, this type of dancing was done mostly in city night clubs frequented by black and Latin teenagers, but after the movie *Saturday Night Fever*, starring John Travolta as an Italian youth from Brooklyn who lived to dance, was released, it became the favorite dance form for white teenagers as well as for adults.

In the 1980s, break dancing achieved great popularity. At first, it was not the type of dancing that everyone could do, as it depended on considerable acrobatic skill. More people watched break dancing performers than attempted to do it themselves. But break dancing was a major cultural phenomenon, and after it had been around a few years, some of its steps were incorporated into other dances. In the late 1980s, even tap dancers started incorporating versions of the Moon Walk into their routines.

Break Dancing

Break dancing started in New York's Harlem and South Bronx areas and in other big-city ghettos in the late 1960s and early 1970s. Its roots were in the black culture's long tradition of public competition to show physical prowess. Back in the 1930s and 1940s, ghetto kids spent a lot of their time tap dancing in the street. In the 1970s, they perfected their disco steps. In the 1980s, they practiced break dancing.

Modern break dancing began as an accompaniment to

"rap music," which is rhythmic, rhyming speech over a heavy beat. Rapping to music began in the 1970s in discos, where disc jockeys started playing around with two or three turntables and a synthesizer. The sound caught on, and soon there were rap records that were played on local radio stations and boomed out of the huge radios that urban youths like to carry around on their shoulders. In fact, it is hard to imagine break dancing ever coming into being without "boom boxes."

The kinds of dances done to rap music were called the Robot, Moon Walk, and Electric Boogie. For the Robot, dancers moved with jerky, mechanical steps. In the Moon Walk, they moved as if in zero gravity, pantomiming the act of walking. The Electric Boogie was similar to the Robot, with machinelike movements. Other routines were combinations of movements like Lofting (diving into the air and landing on the hands with the body still in the air and the legs high), the Bridge (a backward handstand), and the Backspin (spinning on the floor, with the back as a fulcrum). Such routines were done in urban neighborhoods until they caught on elsewhere. In 1972, a group of regular dancers on *Soul Train*, a popular TV show, formed the Lockers, an acrobatic dance group. TV appearances by the Lockers started other kids doing acrobatic dancing.

A disc jockey named Afrika Bambaataa is credited with giving this type of dancing the name "break dancing." As early as 1969, he saw the possibilities for acrobatic dancing to provide healthy competition among street gangs. He called for a "break" in the usual street warfare

188

and suggested that gangs fight with steps rather than with weapons. Still, break dancing might have remained confined to big cities if it hadn't been for two things.

One was the tremendous popularity of Michael Jackson and of the type of dancing he did onstage in concert performances. The other was *Flashdance*, a feature film released nationwide about a girl who wants to dance more than anything else. At the end of the film, she auditions for admission to a ballet school and amazes the staid judges by spinning on her back like a top and doing all sorts of other jazz-dance moves. Not since *Saturday Night Fever* had a film inspired so many moviegoers to dance. Interestingly, while the dancer in *Flashdance* was a woman, most break dancers, especially in the early 1980s, were male.

The success of *Flashdance* spawned two other movies about break dancing—*Breakin'* and *Beat Street*. And because of these films, break dancing made the crossover from black and Hispanic ghetto kids to middle-class kids in the suburbs.

Michael Jackson and Michael Peters

Michael Jackson was a major force in the popularization of break dancing and dancing in general. His idol was Fred Astaire, a white ballroom dancer who made a number of movies with Ginger Rogers in the 1930s and 1940s, and Jackson used a lot of ballroom moves as well as break dancing steps.

In 1974, when he was still with his brothers in the Jackson

Five, the group had a hit record called "Dancin' Machine." In live performances, Michael, who was the star performer of the group, did the Robot when the group sang that song. Several years later, after he left the group and went out on his own, he started doing other dances when he performed, types of dances which by then were called Electric Boogie. When he performed the hit single "Billie Jean" from his 1982 hit album *Thriller*, he did the Moon Walk. In 1983, his video for "Beat It," another hit song from the *Thriller* album, was released. In this video he introduced a new step invented by choreographer Michael Peters called the Worm. It is an undulating, wavelike step done as you back up. In no time, half the kids in America were doing the Worm and the Moon Walk.

But the biggest Michael Jackson video from *Thriller* was yet to come: the video for the title song. Once again, Michael Peters was the choreographer. Peters' style is to move according to the sounds of the instruments in a record; he doesn't use established dance steps and rhythms. Thus, he is a choreographer in the tradition of Buddy Bradley. In this way, the body becomes an echo of the instrument, and in a music video, that was exciting and new. For Michael Jackson, Michael Peters became a new idol—someone he could work with, not just watch in old movies.

The "Thriller" video was the first video that MTV ever actually paid to air. Before that time, videos had been given to MTV, just as records are given to radio stations— the idea being that airtime for records and videos is free advertising and will generate sales for those records. But the "Thriller" video, and other videos that were being

In the age of music videos, choreographers like Michael Peters have become almost as important as the stars themselves. It was Michael Peters who choreographed the Michael Jackson videos "Thriller" and "Beat It." *Author's Collection.*

made by that time, were so sophisticated and so costly to produce that they were really like short films. Michael Jackson thought his videos should be considered films, and that MTV should pay for them.

Videos were still quite new then, but Michael Jackson's videos revolutionized the form. The quality of his productions, and in particular the choreography, put other artists' videos to shame. Soon, other artists were including dance sequences and hiring choreographers to do the dances in their videos.

As for Michael Peters, he went on to co-choreograph the dances for the hit Broadway musical *Dreamgirls*, a thinly disguised story about Diana Ross and the Supremes in their Motown days. In 1984, he won a Tony Award for his work on that show. Later that year, he choreographed the dances for another Broadway show, *Leader of the Pack*.

Almost as popular as *Flashdance* was the movie *Fame*, which was released in 1980. In fact, *Fame* was so popular that it spawned a television series about a special performing arts high school (modeled on Manhattan's High School of the Performing Arts) and the students and teachers there. It was a small role in the film that gave Debbie Allen her first big break.

Debbie Allen

Debbie Allen was born in Houston, Texas, on January 16, 1950, the third of four children.

Allen began taking dance lessons at the age of three, but

it was seeing a performance of Alvin Ailey's ballet *Revelations* that made her determined to be a professional dancer. Her mother tried to enroll her in the Houston Foundation for Ballet when Allen was eight, but she was turned down. Allen believes that the school had a policy of racial segregation and would not admit black students. Instead, Debbie studied privately. She also studied with the Ballet Nacional de Mexico during the year that the family spent in Mexico City. Finally, when she was fourteen, she was admitted to the Houston Foundation for Ballet with a full scholarship, becoming the only black dancer in the company.

As graduation from high school neared, Allen applied to the North Carolina School of the Arts. She was invited for an audition and was even asked to demonstrate her technique to the other young dancers who were auditioning. But she was turned down. The reason given by the school's dance director was that she was "built wrong," but Allen suspected that the real reason was an unofficial racial quota system. It made Allen so bitter that she stopped dancing for a year.

Allen enrolled at Howard University, an all-black school in Washington, D.C., and took courses in Greek classics, speech, and theater arts. She met the choreographer Mike Malone, who persuaded her to resume her dancing and asked her to join his dance troupe. She also danced with student groups at Howard, studied at the National Ballet School, and headed the dance department of what became the Duke Ellington School of the Performing Arts in Washington, D.C.

After graduating with high honors from Howard, Allen

went to New York, where the choreographer Louis Johnson cast her as a dancer in the all-black Broadway musical *Purlie*. After six months with the show, she left to join George Faison's modern dance troupe, The Universal Dance Experience, as a principal dancer. After a year with the Faison troupe, she returned to Broadway, where she got a job in the chorus of the all-black musical *Raisin*. She so distinguished herself as a dancer, however, that soon she was given a major role in the production. She stayed with that show for two years, leaving in 1975. That same year, she married Winfred Wilford, an executive with CBS Records.

For several years after that, Allen held a variety of jobs, appearing in TV commercials, a short-lived TV series called *3 Girls 3*, TV specials on dance, and a made-for-TV movie. In 1979, she played Alex Haley's wife in the special television mini-series, *Roots: The Next Generation*. Meanwhile, she had worked on the stage from time to time, but the shows were either revivals of old productions or new productions that were unsuccessful. Her best stage role came in 1979, when she replaced Charlene Woodard in the musical *Ain't Misbehavin'*.

Finally, in 1980, she got the kind of role she had been waiting for, playing Anita in a Broadway revival of *West Side Story*. Critics gave her rave reviews, and she was nominated for a Tony Award and received the Drama Desk Award.

The role that made her famous came about around the same time. In the movie *Fame*, she was cast as a dance instructor, a bit part in which she only said two lines.

But once writers began to work on a TV series based on the movie, the part of the dance instructor, Lydia Grant, became a major one. The producers of the series wanted Allen for the role, but she was reluctant to devote so much of her time to TV and took the job only on the condition that she get to choreograph all the dances for the series. She got what she wanted, and became the moving force behind the series.

At the end of its first season, *Fame* won five Emmy Awards, including one to Debbie Allen for choreography. She won the award again after the second season. By 1984, she was one of the show's producers, and in 1985–1986 she directed several of the episodes.

Allen and her husband Winfred Wilford were divorced in 1983. The following year, she married Norm Nixon, a basketball player with the San Diego Clippers. They have a daughter named Vivian.

Meanwhile, she appeared in a made-for-TV movie called *Women of San Quentin* and co-wrote, choreographed, and performed in a TV special called *Dancin' in the Wings*, which also featured Sammy Davis, Jr. In 1986, she appeared in the Richard Pryor movie *Jo Jo Dancer, Your Life Is Calling*.

She finally returned to Broadway in 1985 in *Sweet Charity*, a revival of a 1966 production, and was credited by most critics with making the show. At the Tony Awards, the show itself won the award for Best Revival, and Allen was nominated as Best Actress in a Musical.

In the fall of 1988, the popular *Cosby Show*, in which Allen's sister Phylicia Rashad co-stars, featured a different opening, one in which the stars of the show dance to

Debbie Allen rehearsing with Gwen Verdon in Los Angeles for the 1985 revival of *Sweet Charity*, for which Allen received a Tony nomination. *PMK Public Relations*.

the theme song. Debbie Allen choreographed the dance sequences. She also produced the spinoff from the *Cosby Show*, *A Different World*.

Despite discrimination, Debbie Allen has made it not only in the field she wanted to—musical comedy—but in other fields as well.

Tap dancing enjoyed a resurgence during the 1970s and 1980s. One reason was the success of the show *Bubblin' Brown Sugar* on Broadway. Still another was the film *The Cotton Club*, which was filled with jazz dancing, especially tap, and whose tap dance consultant, Henri LeTang, had been a tap coach on Broadway years before. Suddenly, old-timers who hadn't been called upon to tap dance in years were in great demand for television specials on tap and as teachers of the form to new dancers. The Nicholas Brothers found themselves working together again. Honi Coles got a featured role in the Broadway show *My One and Only*, starring Twiggy and Tommy Tune, and won a Tony Award.

In January 1989, a new Broadway show called *Black and Blue* featured blues and jazz music and singing, and a heavy concentration of tap. Veterans Henri LeTang, Cholly Atkins (Honi Coles' partner in Coles and Atkins), and Fayard Nicholas did the choreography. The following month, the Hollywood film *Tap* opened. It was written and directed by Nick Castle, whose father had choreographed for Fred Astaire, Gene Kelly, and the Nicholas Brothers back in the 1940s. Its supporting cast included Harold Nicholas and other veteran hoofers like Sandman Sims and Bunny Briggs. Sammy Davis, Jr., and Gregory

Hines co-starred, and the movie created such excitement when it opened in New York that Mayor Edward Koch declared the week of February 6, 1989, Tap Week in New York. It seemed that tap was finally back.

By the time he appeared in *Tap*, Gregory Hines was one of the best-known male popular dancers of the 1980s. Earlier in the decade, he had starred in *The Cotton Club* movie and with Mikhail Baryshnikov, the Russian-born ballet dancer, in the film *White Nights*. The 1980s were actually the time of his "second career" as a tap dancer, for he was tapping on stages when he was a child.

Gregory Hines

Gregory Hines was born February 14, 1946, in New York City, the second son of Maurice Hines, Sr., and Alma Iola Lawless Hines. The Hines family has a show-business background—their grandmother had been a showgirl at the Cotton Club, and their father had worked as a nightclub bouncer. Gregory and his older brother, Maurice, were steered into tap dancing by their mother, who was a great admirer of the Nicholas Brothers and hoped her sons might become a successful tap dancing act. She often took them to the Apollo Theater in Harlem so they could watch professional tap dancers.

By the time Gregory was five, he and Maurice, who were billed as the Hines Kids, were performing at local talent shows. By the time he was six, they had debuted at the Apollo, causing such a stir that they were held over for a total of two weeks. When he was eight, they

Gregory (left) and Maurice Hines started dancing professionally when they were youngsters. *Museum of the City of New York.*

were cast in a Broadway musical called *The Girl in Pink Tights*, which unfortunately soon closed. By this time, however, they had met Henri LeTang, a choreographer and tap coach for Broadway dancers, and under his guidance they became internationally known tap dancing stars.

When Maurice reached his teens, the term "Kids" didn't fit anymore, so the brothers became the Hines Brothers. For a brief period, they took on a third member of the team, a singer and pantomimist named Johnny Brown, and became Hines, Hines, and Brown. They were still traveling internationally, chaperoned by their mother, but in the early 1960s, their father was tired of being left behind by his family. So Maurice, Sr., took up the drums and in 1963 joined the act, which now became Hines, Hines, and Dad.

At this time, tap dancing was out of style, so the brothers switched to comedy. Gregory was the comedian, Maurice the straight man, and their father the percussionist. They were successful in this guise and performed repeatedly on *The Ed Sullivan Show* and *The Tonight Show*. They also continued their success in Europe, playing London and Paris clubs. After ten years, however, the interests of the two brothers diverged, and in 1973, the Hines act disbanded. Maurice pursued a career in theater. Gregory, who had been strongly influenced by the 1960s counterculture, underwent major changes in his life. He divorced his wife, Patricia, a dance therapist, moved to Venice, California, grew his hair long, and formed a jazz-rock group called Severance. He also worked as a waiter, busboy, and karate instructor. While in Venice, he met and married his second wife, Pamela Koslow.

When their father, a drummer, joined the Hines Brothers, the act became known as Hines, Hines, and Dad. *Museum of the City of New York*.

After five years as a self-proclaimed "California hippie," Gregory, with his second wife, moved back to New York so that he could be close to his daughter from his first marriage, Daria. On the same day he arrived in the city, his brother Maurice told him about an audition for a revue called *The Last Minstrel Show*. Gregory had to buy a pair of tap shoes for the audition, but even though he was rusty, he landed a part. The revue opened and closed in Philadelphia, and never made it to Broadway, but it gave Gregory Hines a chance to get back into tap dancing.

Later in 1978, both Gregory and Maurice starred in the musical tribute to the composer Eubie Blake *Eubie!*, whose tap sequences were choreographed by their old teacher, Henri LeTang. They were hailed for their performances, and Gregory, who also sang in the show, was credited with giving the show most of its humor. He won an Outer Critics' Circle Award as outstanding featured performer in a musical and was nominated for a Tony Award in the same category. It is generally agreed that *Eubie!* and the tap dancing in the show clinched tap dancing's return to popularity after a hiatus of many years.

Gregory's next project was a film called *Comin' Uptown*, a Broadway musical-comedy version of *A Christmas Carol* set in Harlem. Playing the role of Scrooge, he did his first real acting, as well as singing and dancing. While the show itself was unsuccessful, Gregory's performance was critically praised, and he received his second straight Tony nomination, this time for outstanding actor in a musical.

In 1980, Hines choreographed *Blues in the Night*, an off-Broadway show, and appeared in *Black Broadway*, a tribute to the black Broadway musicals of the past, with Charles "Honi" Coles, John Bubbles (of the famous tap dancing team of Buck and Bubbles), Nell Carter, and others. Later that year, he headed the cast of *Sophisticated Ladies*, which also starred Judith Jamison. Donald McKayle directed and choreographed the show, while Henri LeTang specifically choreographed tap sequences. During tryouts of the show in Philadelphia, reviewers complained that the show did not feature the talents of Hines and Jamison enough, but McKayle did not alter the show. When the show moved to Washington, D.C., Hines made similar complaints and was fired from the show. Other cast members supported him, however, and he was rehired. Michael Smuin replaced Donald McKayle as director. Smuin redid the entire show, emphasizing music and dance over story line, and in this form it was a major hit on Broadway, running for two years. Hines received his third straight Tony nomination.

After he had been with the show for a year, Gregory turned his role over to Maurice in order to head the West Coast production of *Sophisticated Ladies*. He wanted to be on the West Coast because of his increasing involvement with movies. In 1981, he appeared in Mel Brooks' *History of the World—Part I*, replacing popular comedian Richard Pryor. Replacing Pryor was difficult, but Hines got excellent reviews in the film. During the next two years, he played a medical examiner in the horror film *Wolfen* and a test pilot in *Deal of the Century*, with Chevy Chase.

Learning that producer Robert Evans intended to make a movie about the Cotton Club, Hines actively sought the role of "Sandman" Williams, a character based on the famous tap dancer Sandman Sims. Once Hines landed the role, he contributed much to the creation of the character. Francis Ford Coppola, scenarist and director of the film, decided to hire Maurice Hines and adapt the story of the Hines brothers' real break-up to the movie. While the film *The Cotton Club* suffered from an identity crisis—half gangster film, half dance film—Gregory Hines received critical praise for his work in it.

Hines' next film was *White Nights*, in which he played a disenchanted American tap dancer who defected to Russia, with Mikhail Baryshnikov as a Russian ballet dancer who had emigrated from the Soviet Union. At this writing, he intends to continue film work and would like to star in a screen biography of Bill "Bojangles" Robinson.

Gregory Hines, and to a lesser extent his brother Maurice, remains the only well-known tap dancer who is not in his seventies. As the old hoofers die out, the Hines brothers will be able to continue the tradition of tap and provide role models for younger dancers. Because he is a talented actor in both dramatic and comedy roles, Gregory Hines has also done much for black dance, in general, by working toward its acceptance in modern films.

During the 1970s and 1980s, concert dance was alive and well, with the most notable groups being the veterans—the Alvin Ailey troupe in modern dance and Dance Theater of Harlem in ballet, which in 1988 celebrated their thirtieth and twentieth anniversaries respectively. But dozens of other troupes sprang up. What marked the 1970s and 1980s was the great variety of dance groups, black and white, national and international, representing all types of dance styles, that could be found touring the United States and abroad.

The Brooklyn Academy of Music, with its emphasis on experimentation in its New Wave and Next Wave festivals, introduced many new dance groups. In black dance, one of the most successful programs has been the annual spring event called Danceafrica, which combines rousing dance and music performances by African and African-American dance groups. There's even an African bazaar in the Academy's parking lot. Started in 1977, the festival featured only African-American groups until its tenth-anniversary celebration in 1987. Beginning in 1988, African dance groups have been included as well. At the festival held in the spring of 1988, the dance groups featured included Urban Bush Women, a New York-based, all-female group; Sabar Ak Ru Afriq, an African-American group; and the Guirivoires from the Ivory Coast.

The annual summer Jacob's Pillow Dance Festival in Lee, Massachusetts, celebrates cultural intermingling in its programs. In 1987, it presented "The Dance and Music of Africa." The program featured various groups of African or African-trained American performers, including the Swazi Women Singers and Dancers, a group of professional weavers from Swaziland; the Ladzekpo Brothers; and the African Music and Dance Ensemble. The 1988 program emphasized the dances of Brazil and the Portuguese and African influences upon these dances. The group Pauliteiros of Cercio, an all-male company from a village in northeastern Portugal, and Roots of Brazil, a New York-based company, were featured.

The Dance Theater of Harlem has offered an annual

205

Arts Exposure Program since 1972 to New York City schoolchildren, at which it has often featured African dance troupes. The featured group at the June 1988 program were the Amabutho Zulu Warriors, who were traveling with the Ringling Brothers and Barnum & Bailey Circus at the time.

In 1988, Atlanta hosted the first of what was planned to be a biennial event called The National Black Arts Festival. The art of dance was well represented by the Alvin Ailey company.

The North Carolina Dance Theater, based in Winston-Salem, has as its principal dancer Mel A. Tomlinson. Born in Raleigh, North Carolina, in 1954, he migrated to New York to pursue his career in dance and was highly successful there. During fifteen years in New York, he danced with Alvin Ailey, Dance Theatre of Harlem (1974–1981), and the New York City Ballet (1981–1987). He graduated from North Carolina School of the Arts, also in Winston-Salem, the same school to which Debbie Allen had been denied admission a few years earlier.

The American Dance Festival

The American Dance Festival at Duke University in North Carolina is another major dance festival that has shown an increasing awareness of the importance of intercultural offerings. It was founded in 1948, when modern dance was still a maverick art, and grew out of the annual summer dance festival held at Bennington College in Vermont. By the close of World War II, the Bennington festival had outgrown the theatrical facilities of the college, and a change in the college's academic calendar meant that more people would be on campus in the summertime, competing for limited space and facilities. The American Dance Festival began at Connecticut College for Women in New London. Although it was not literally a continuation of the Bennington festival, it was clearly inspired by and modeled after it; and its founders were former dancers or teachers at Bennington. Directed by Martha Hill and Ruth Bloomer, the school was called the Connecticut College School of the Dance, and the series of public performances that occurred in the summer were called the American Dance Festival.

The first summer festival featured three modern dance companies that could be said to represent the liveliest trends in the form at the time. They were the Martha Graham company; a company jointly directed by Jane Dudley, Sophie Maslow, and William Bales; and the José Limón company, whose founder, director, and choreographer was Mexican born.

In 1950, Pearl Primus introduced black dance to the festival, though not entirely successfully. Critics called her presentations "uneven." Not for another ten years would ethnic dance be considered seriously. In 1960, the festival included a program of dances from Korea, Argentina, Japan, Spain, Jamaica, and Haiti by foreign students. No black "name" modern dancers were represented. The following year La Meri, a Spanish dancer, served as the major ethnic dance component.

Finally, at the fifteenth-anniversary festival in 1962, Alvin Ailey was one of thirteen choreographers whose work was presented; and from then on, black choreographers and dance companies became a regular part of the festival's offerings, reflecting in part the coming of age of black modern dance and in part the maturing of white society—or at least artistic society—concerning the talents of blacks. Donald McKayle and the Haitian dancer Jean-Leon Destine were invited to the 1963 festival, where McKayle's *Arena* premiered. The increased inclusion of "ethnic" dancing did not go unnoticed. Allen Hughes, who became the chief dance critic for *The New York Times* on John Martin's retirement, remarked that while the festival had occasionally taken note of "ethnic" dance, it was still ignoring ballet. It is unlikely that Hughes' assertion had anything to do with the fact that for the next six years no "ethnic" dancers or choreographers were represented at the festival, with the exception of Japanese ones.

It was not just black and other ethnic dancers and choreographers who were being left out. Many white dancers and choreographers were never invited to the festival. In fact, by the time the festival celebrated its twentieth anniversary, some critics were charging that it was "stuffy," which was serious criticism indeed of a festival that prided itself on its modern dance as modern art. Allen Hughes wrote in 1964 that the festival "has systematically, if subtly, focused attention upon one set of dance people [referring to Martha Graham, Doris Humphrey, and José Limón] at the expense of others who, though perhaps not part of the set, have been making equal (sometimes greater) contributions to the vitality of modern dance in America."

Charles Reinhart took over as director of the American Dance Festival in 1969 and immediately started to bring in "new blood." In fact, sometimes critics said his festivals were like smorgasbords, meaning that they included a little bit of everything. This was not always a positive statement, for sometimes critics complained that the festivals had no focus. Still, a smorgasbord was better than the old "one-course meals" in the eyes of black dancers. That summer, both Talley Beatty and Alvin Ailey premiered new works—*Bring My Servant Home* and *Masekela Language*. Talley Beatty was also hired to teach a course in jazz dance at the school. Ailey returned for the twenty-fifth-anniversary festival in 1972, and the following year, 1973, both Donald McKayle's Los Angeles-based Inner City Dance Company and Arthur Mitchell's Dance Theater of Harlem participated, one of the few times that ballet was represented at the festival.

In 1974, the six-year-old Chuck Davis Dance Company appeared at the festival for the first time, participating in the scholarship program, which became an international event with the participation of Indian and Spanish companies. Born in Raleigh, North Carolina, in 1937, Davis had become involved in dance while serving in the Navy and had trained with the Klara Harrington Dance Theater in Washington, D.C., while attending Howard University. He performed with the dance troupes accompanying percussionist Olatunji and vocalist Miriam Makeba and with the concert groups of Eleo Pomare, Raymond Sawyer, Bernice Johnson, and Joan Miller. In 1968, he formed his own company and choreographed many pieces for them, but became equally well known for his work in the staging of portions of dances and rituals from many areas of Africa for his company. He and his company were back in 1975, along with Dance Theater of Harlem and Alvin Ailey's Junior Company, and again in 1976. That same year, Judith Jamison, as guest artist with American Dance Machine, performed *Cry*, Alvin Ailey's tribute to black women. In 1977, Dance Theater of Harlem and Carmen De Lavallade and Company performed at the festival.

Meanwhile, however, the festival staff and college officials had not been getting along, and the festival administration had charged both the college and the surrounding New London community with not giving it enough support. After several years of strained relations, the American Dance Festival decided to move. Its new home would be the campus of Duke University in Durham, North Carolina.

The Philadelphia-based Arthur Hall Afro-American Dance Ensemble performed at the premier festival at Duke. The Alvin Ailey company performed the following year. In 1980, the festival featured a program of jazz and jazz dance that included performances by Honi Coles and the trumpeter Dizzy Gillespie. The 1981 festival featured the Chuck Davis company, Dance Theater of Harlem, and works by five young choreographers, including *Social Intercourse* by Bill T. Jones, which was performed to music supplied by a "ghetto-blaster" portable radio.

By this time, Chuck Davis was associated with ADF in an official capacity, as director of the festival's Community Services Program. He emphasized the communal nature

210

of his work *Rites of Passage* by including members of the Durham community, among them his eighty-two-year-old father, in the cast. In 1983, he brought African dance to the festival, organizing Festival Africa, three nights of African dance and music. It was the first festival of its kind in the Southeast and featured performances by American companies specializing in African dance and by African-born dancers living in the United States. The participants included Kombo Omolara; Olukose Wiles; Art of Black Dance and Music; Chuck Davis' own company, which by now was called the African-American Dance Ensemble; Calabash Dance Company; Weaver Street Dancers; the Cultural Movement; and Dinizulu and His African Dancers, Drummers, and Singers.

In 1985, Davis' community-based African-American Dance Ensemble, composed of dancers who danced only in their free time, staged the premiere of *Saturday Night/ Sunday Morning*.

In 1987, the American Dance Festival began a three-year project called "The Black Tradition in American Modern Dance." Supported by the Ford Foundation and the National Endowment for the Humanities, it included seminars on dance by black choreographers, archival recordings of their works, and the publication of a collection of essays bearing the same title as the project. The culminating event in the first year of the project took place in June, at the annual festival, in a program that featured the work of four black choreographers. The Joel Hall Dancers did Talley Beatty's "Congo Tango Palace," from his *Come and Get the Beauty of It Hot*. Eleo Pomare was

211

represented by his 1967 *Desenamoradas*, danced by the Dayton Contemporary Dance Company to music by John Coltrane. Donald McKayle's *Games*, performed by the Chuck Davis African-American Dance Ensemble, was another program highlight. The event was rounded out with three solos choreographed by Pearl Primus—*The Negro Speaks of Rivers*, "Strange Fruit," and *Hard Times Blues*, danced by Kim Y. Bears and Warren T. Miller.

The innovations and program variety of the American Dance Festival in North Carolina—a non–New York site—are becoming more and more typical of dance in the United States. Not just black dance, but all dance, particularly modern dance. Most dancers and dance insiders agree that dance has reached its peak in the twentieth century. They also agree that the pioneering era is ending. The founders of the country's major modern dance and ballet companies have died or are less active than in the past. The dance is moving away from its New York center, and the number of regional companies outside New York is burgeoning. One example among many is Garth Fagan's Bucket Dance Theater, based in Rochester, New York. There are also fewer distinctions between ballet and modern dance, and groups that follow one or the other style are less divided and hostile toward one another.

Mel Tomlinson, for one, thinks it is healthy that dancers are going out to regional companies. "Dancers are leaving New York because they believe in what they're going toward," he says. "Until recently there weren't any companies worth leaving for. But there is a great deal of dance activity spreading out now. People want to settle

212

down to have something to call *theirs*, financially and family-wise. They are leaving what we call major dance companies—and since these are major people who are leaving, the companies they are going to are also becoming major. . . ."

While black dancers have become more acceptable, issues of race still exist. Only in modern dance is casting done largely without regard to color or physical characteristics. In the theater, and in ballet, things still have a long way to go. In New York, these problems are perhaps magnified because of that city's premiere position in American theater and dance. The fact remains, however, that on Broadway the best chances for black dancers are in black shows. There were no blacks in the major shows of 1988, such as *Phantom of the Opera, Les Miserables,* or *Me and My Girl.* The argument that these are British productions does not stand up, since *Cats* and *Starlight Express* were also British productions and they did include minority performers. A black woman still cannot get a job in the long-running show *A Chorus Line.* In the fall of 1988, Jerome Robbins came under fire for not hiring blacks for the cast of fifty dancers in his upcoming show *Jerome Robbins' Broadway.* Only after a complaint from a representative of the show business union Actors' Equity did he hire one black dancer who would perform when a cast member was sick or injured.

Not until 1988 was a black dancer finally hired by the Rockettes—the first since New York City's Radio City Music Hall opened in December 1932. And minority representation in the New York City Ballet, the American

213

Ballet Theatre, and the Joffrey Ballet is token at best. The argument that blacks simply don't look right in classical ballets cannot be made in this case, because the major part of the repertoires of the New York City Ballet and the Joffrey are nontraditional ballets where conformity to a physical type is less important than in nineteenth-century ballets.

Opera companies, which in some ways present a more conservative art form, have a better record than ballet companies and Broadway in casting black singers without regard to their color. Shirley Verrett, for example, can sing any role to which her voice is suited and is not regarded as a "black opera singer."

In an editorial in *The New York Times* in January 1988, David Vaughan, archivist of the Cunningham Dance Foundation, pointed out, "In Jennifer Dunning's history of the School of American Ballet, *But First a School*, part of the original plan in 1933 was for the student body to include eight white and eight black youngsters. The idea was soon forgotten, but if it had been pursued, American ballet might look very different today. It might look the way one would want it to look: a reflection of the real world around us."

Until that day comes, black dancers can take heart in the knowledge that some of the most respected dancers in the twentieth century recognize how vital has been the role of black dance in modern America and, indeed, the world. In her 1963 *Book of the Dance*, the choreographer Agnes de Mille wrote, "Since 1850 there has been little change in [dance in] Europe. All further innovations have

214

come from the United States, Cuba, or South America, and all broke with previous tradition." One of the primary sources of these innovations, especially the rhythms, has been Africa, and the messengers of those rhythms have been black people.

Selected Bibliography

Anderson, Jack. *The American Dance Festival*. Durham, NC: Duke University Press, 1987.

Cohen-Stratyner, Barbara Naomi. *Biographical Dictionary of Dance*. New York: G. Schirmer, Inc., 1982.

de Mille, Agnes. *America Dances*. New York: The Macmillan Company, 1980.

Emery, Lynne Fauley. *Black Dance in the United States from 1619 to 1970*. Palo Alto, CA: National Press Books, 1972.

Haskins, James. *About Michael Jackson*. Hillside, NJ: Enslow Publishers, 1985.

_____. *Black Music in America: A History Through Its People*. New York: Thomas Y. Crowell, 1987.

_____. *Black Theater in America*. New York: Thomas Y. Crowell, 1982.

_____. *Break Dancing*. Minneapolis, MN: Lerner Publications Co., 1985.

_____. *The Cotton Club*. New York: New American Library, 1984.

_____. *Katherine Dunham*. New York: Coward, McCann & Geoghegan, Inc., 1982.

_____, and N. R. Mitgang. *Mr. Bojangles: The Biography of Bill Robinson*. New York: William Morrow and Company, 1988.

216

Hodgson, Moira. *Quintet: Five American Dance Companies*. Photographs by Thomas Victor. New York: William Morrow and Company, 1976.

Hughes, Langston. *The Big Sea*. New York: Hill & Wang, Inc., 1940.

_____, and Milton Meltzer. *Black Magic: A Pictorial History of the Negro in American Entertainment*. Englewood Cliffs, NJ: Prentice-Hall, Inc., 1967.

Johnson, James Weldon. *Black Manhattan*. New York: Alfred A. Knopf, Inc., 1930.

Kimball, Robert, and William Bolcom. *Reminiscing with Sissle and Blake*. New York: The Viking Press, Inc., 1973.

Lewis, Roscoe. *The Negro in Virginia*. New York: Arno Press, 1969.

Martin, John. *John Martin's Book of the Dance*. New York: Tudor Publishing Co., 1963.

Maynard, Olga. *Judith Jamison: Aspects of a Dancer*. New York: Doubleday & Company, Inc., 1982.

McDonagh, Don. *The Complete Guide to Modern Dance*. Garden City, NY: Doubleday & Company, Inc., 1976.

Parrish, Lydia. *Slave Songs of the Georgia Sea Islands*. Hatboro, PA: Folklore Associates, 1965.

Schoener, Allon, ed. *Harlem on My Mind: Cultural Capital of Black America 1900–1968*. New York: Random House, Inc., 1968.

Sobel, Mechal. *The World They Made Together: Black and White Values in Eighteenth-Century Virginia*. Princeton, NJ: Princeton University Press, 1987.

Stearns, Marshal and Jean. *Jazz Dance: The Story of American Vernacular Dance*. New York: The Macmillan Company, 1968.

Stuckey, Sterling. *Slave Culture: Nationalist Theory and the Foundations of Black America*. New York: Oxford University Press, 1987.

Terry, Walter. *The Dance in America*. New York: Harper & Row, Publishers, 1956.

Selected Videography

African and Ethnic Dance

Studies in Nigerian Dance, No. 1: TIV Division (1966, 12 minutes, black and white, 16mm film) Three complete Icough dances are performed by the women ensembles of Alide village, illustrating new and traditional forms and a number of variations of the Icough movements.

Studies in Nigerian Dance, No. 2: Jos Plateau (10 minutes, black and white, 16mm film) Shows 5 dances as performed by men of the Iriwge people of the Jos Plateau. Highlights specific movements as well as the ensemble, which consists of singers, drummers, and dancers.

Both available for rental through University of California, Los Angeles, Instructional Media Library, Powell Library—Room 46, Los Angeles, CA 90024   (213) 825–0755

Chuck Davis: Dancing Through West Africa (28 minutes, color, 16mm film or video) Chuck Davis takes several members of his troupe on a visit to West African villages to learn the local dances.

Available for rental through Filmmakers Library, 124 East 40th Street, New York, NY 10016   (212) 808–4980

Dance Like a River: Odadaa! Drumming and Dancing in the U.S. (45 minutes, color, 16mm film or video) Documents the dance styles, purpose, and several performances of Odadaa!, a Ga dance company from Ghana, West Africa, that now makes its home in Washington, DC.

Ethnic Dance—Roundtrip to Trinidad (29 minutes, black and white, 16mm film or video) Presents a variety of West Indian dances and explains their derivations and movements. Includes "Bele," a West Indian adaptation of the minuet; "Yanvallou," a voodoo dance; and "Banda," a Haitian dance about death. Features Geoffrey Holder and Carmen De Lavallade.

Both available for rental or purchase through Indiana University Audio-Visual Center, Bloomington, IN 47405   (812) 855–8087

Tap Dancing and Jazz

No Maps on My Taps (58 minutes, color, 16mm film or video) The spirit of tap in its heyday, shown in rare photos and Hollywood film clips of the 1930s. Sandman Sims, Chuck Green, and Bunny Buggs tell the story of tap as an expression of black heritage and culture.

Available for rental or purchase through Direct Cinema Limited, P.O. Box 69589, Los Angeles, CA 90069   (213) 656–4700

Songs Unwritten: A Tap Dancer Remembered (58 minutes, color, video) A portrait of tap dancer Leon Collins, including interviews and performances to jazz and classical music.

Available for purchase through Leon Collins Archive, P.O. Box 28128, Philadelphia, PA 19131

Tap Dancin' (58 minutes, color, 16mm film or video) Explores the art of American jazz dance through stage performances, interviews, and vintage film clips of Bill "Bojangles" Robinson, The Four Step Brothers, Honi Coles and Cholly Atkins, and The Nicholas Brothers. New performances by The Hoofers, Jazz Tap Ensemble, The Copasetics, Third Generation Step,

John Bubbles, Honi Coles, Fayard and Harold Nicholas, Phil Black and his students, and Marco Anderson of the original Four Step Brothers.
Available for rental through Blackwood Productions, Inc., 251 West 57th Street, New York, NY 10019   (212) 247–4710

In-Jazz Way: A Portrait of Mura Dehn (30 minutes, color, 16mm film or video) An account of black social dance during the 30s and 40s with film clips of Harlem's Savoy Ballroom.

Call of the Jitterbug (35 minutes, color, video) Explores the Jitterbug/Lindy Hop dance craze through interviews with musicians and dancers who performed in Harlem's Savoy Ballroom.
Both available for rental or purchase through Filmmakers Library, 124 East 40th Street, New York, NY 10016   (212) 808–4980

Dance Black America (90 minutes, color, 16mm film or video) The Black Dance America Festival presented by the Brooklyn Academy of Music and State University of New York in 1983. Film includes performances by the Alvin Ailey American Dance Theatre, Lindy Hopping by Mama LaParks Jazz Dancers, Charles Moore in Asadata Dafora's "Ostrich," Leon Jackson as Master Juba, and Al Derryman as "Snakehips" Tucker.
Available for rental through Pennebaker Associates, Inc., 21 West 86th Street, New York, NY 10024   (212) 496–9195

Modern Dance and Ballet

Carnival of Rhythm (20 minutes, black and white, 16mm film) Choreographed and performed by Katherine Dunham.
Available for rental through Dance Films Association, Inc., Room 507, 1133 Broadway, New York, NY 10010   (212) 727–0764

Dance Theater of Harlem (60 minutes, color, 16mm film or video) Features members of the Dance Theater of Harlem as they

220

appear informally and in rehearsal and perform selections from their repertoire, including "Forces of Rhythm," "Do the Breakdown," "He Ain't Heavy, He's My Brother," "Bugaku," "The Beloved," the "Holberg Suite," and "Dougla."
Available for rental or purchase through Indiana University Audio-Visual Center, Bloomington, IN 47405   (812) 855–8087

Rhythmetron: The Dance Theater of Harlem with Arthur Mitchell (52 minutes, color, 16mm film) Views practice sessions, demonstrations, and performances of Arthur Mitchell's Dance Theater of Harlem from 1973. Filmed in a Harlem church basement used as a studio, and before an audience of Philadelphia schoolchildren, the performances show the application of ballet movements to three styles of dance: classical, neoclassical, and a combination of African, Jazz, and modern movements. Includes excerpts from Mitchell's "Fête Noire," "Biosfera," and "Rhythmetron."
Available for rental from Pennsylvania State University Audio-Visual Services, Special Services Building, University Park, PA 16802   (814) 865–6314

Stravinsky's Firebird by Dance Theatre of Harlem (60 minutes, color, video) Rehearsal of Stravinsky's *Firebird*. Geoffrey Holder, the costume and set designer, talks about his designs.
Produced by WQED, Pittsburgh, and the John F. Kennedy Center for the Performing Arts, and available for purchase through WQED Pittsburgh, 4802 Fifth Avenue, Pittsburgh, PA 15213

Ailey Dances (85 minutes, color, video) Features four of his most critically acclaimed works: "Cry," "The Lark Ascending," "Revelations," and "Night Creatures." Recorded live at New York's City Center, with introductions by former Ailey star Judith Jamison.
Available for purchase through Kultur Performing Arts Video cassettes, 121 Highway 36, W. Long Branch, NJ 07764   (201) 229–2343

An Evening with the Alvin Ailey American Dance Theater (108 minutes, color, video) Includes performances of "Divining," "Revelations," "The Stack-Up," and "Cry."
Available for purchase through Home Vision, 5547 N. Ravenswood Avenue, Chicago, IL 60640   (800) 826–3456

Alvin Ailey: Memories and Visions (1974, 54 minutes, color, 16mm film or video) Produced by WNET/Thirteen; includes excerpts from "Blues Suite," "The Lark Ascending," "Mary Lou's Mass," "Cry" performed by Judith Jamison, "A Song for You," "Hidden Rites," and "Revelations."
Available for rental or purchase from Phoenix/BFA films, 470 Park Avenue South, New York, NY 10016   (212) 684–5910

Dancemaker (30 minutes, color, video) An anatomy of a modern dance production, *Dancemaker* follows choreographer Judith Jamison and her troupe from first auditions to opening night of "With Us," a world premiere celebrating the newly formed University of the Arts.
Available through WHYY-TV12, Attn: Art Ellis, 150 N. Sixth Street, Philadelphia, PA 19106   (215) 351–1200

Lemonade Suite (30 minutes, color, video) An interpretation through music and dance of the works of black poet Gwendolyn Brooks. Choreography by Iris Rosa, Director of the Indiana University Afro-American Dance Company.
Available for rental or purchase through Indiana University Audio-Visual Center, Bloomington, IN 47405   (812) 855–5087

Grateful acknowledgment is made to Susan Braun of Dance Films Association, 1133 Broadway, Room 507, New York, NY 10010, for her help in compiling this videography.

Index

Numbers in *italics* refer to illustrations.

225

229

231

232

DATE DUE
